Online Education:
6 Steps to Starting an Online School

D. KENT MULFORD, D.O., MBA

ONLINE EDUCATION:

6 STEPS TO STARTING AN ONLINE SCHOOL

BookSurge Publishing
2005

Online Education:
6 Steps to Starting an Online School

ACKNOWLEDGMENTS

P roducing a guide that would cover the basics of starting and running an online graduate school seemed at first an onerous undertaking to me. Without the encouragement and help of several people, it is doubtful I would have ever written the first word.

To Dr. Michael Creedon I owe my gratitude for having provided much of the information on geriatric health management in Appendix E. Dr. Creedon, a distinguished educator and author, is the president of The Creedon Group in Vienna, Virginia. He also coordinates the Certificate on Aging Studies Program at The Johns Hopkins University and serves as a professor of geriatric health management at A.T. Still University of Health Sciences in Kirksville, Missouri.

Dr. Creedon has held numerous other posts, including director of aging research for Carlow International, Inc., 1993-2000, and director of corporate programs for the National Council on the Aging, 1987-90. He was also the Virginia Prentice Andrews Chair in Gerontology at the University of Bridgeport, 1984-87. Previously, he taught at the Catholic University of America School of Social Service, 1979-1984. His publications include *Selected Readings in Assessment and Case Management* (co-editor, published by the District of Columbia Office on Aging, 1983); *Issues for an Aging America: Employees and Eldercare* (editor and senior author, published by the University of Bridgeport, 1987); *Managing Work and Family Life* (co-author, published by

Springer Press, 1994); and *A Study of Safety and Quality of Life in Long-Term Care Facilities* (co-author, published by the Western Health Board of Ireland, 1999).

In 1995, Dr. Creedon was a delegate and section leader for the White House Conference on Aging. That same year, he keynoted the White House Mini-Conference on Eldercare, and he was co-manager of the White House Mini-Conference on Transportation and the Elderly. More recently, he chaired the Home Environment section of the Fairfax County, Virginia, Task Force on Long-Term Care (final report submitted in March 2002). He is presently the senior research scientist for "ADEPT: A Nurse Aide ADL Computerized Training Tool for Nursing Homes," a project sponsored by Carlow International, Inc., with funding from the National Institutes of Health.

I also thank Michael Samuels, Dr.P.H., for writing the Introduction. Dr. Samuels is the Distinguished Scholar and Endowed Chair in Rural Health Policy and professor of family practice and community medicine at the University of Kentucky College of Medicine. He previously was chair of the Department of Health Administration at the University of South Carolina's Arnold School of Public Health. While at South Carolina, he developed the Master's in Health Administration (MHA) program, which was soon accredited by the Accrediting Commission on Education for Health Services Administration. He also directed the Master's in Public Health (MPH) program and saw it through two accreditation reviews by the Council on Education for Public Health. Later he developed the MHA and MPH programs for the School of Health Management at A.T. Still University of Health Sciences, and he continues to direct these programs.

I also wish to acknowledge my editor, Bob Lofft. Working from his home office in Eugene, Oregon, Bob took my

rather matter-of-fact writing style and gave it coherence and readability. He made me appear a better writer than I am, and he did it in record time.

The reviewer of my final draft, Dr. Fred Pugh, also deserves my special thanks. As his former student, I knew I could count on him to tell me where my inconsistencies were and recommend cures for them.

Most of all, I want to thank my son Darren. He gave me the push I needed to make the attempt at writing this book, and it is because of him that you are reading it now. Darren, besides inspiring me, was also my graphic designer. He spent long hours working on the cover and, when he finished, his design truly captured the essence of this book.

— D. Kent Mulford, D.O., M.B.A.

INTRODUCTION

In 2002 the Institute of Medicine (IOM) of the National Academy of Sciences published *The Future of the Public's Health in the 21st Century.* This report enlarged upon IOM's landmark 1988 report, *The Future of Public Health.* The focus of that report was on ways to strengthen the infrastructure supporting the government's role in ensuring the public's health.

The more recent 2002 report addresses the concerns of the 1988 report in light of present realities, and it offers recommendations not only on the role of government, but also on the roles of higher education, business, health care delivery systems, community organizations, and the media. In this seminal work, IOM with its 34 recommendations has set the tone for the national reform of public health.

One of the more alarming findings of the 1988 report was that over 80 percent of the public health workforce lacked formal training in public health. The 2002 report again cites lack of training as a threat to the integrity of the public health system. At a time marked by terrorism and natural disasters, this is a chilling thought.

Many of our country's local health departments are physically distant from universities that offer graduate training in public health. Additionally, our rural hospitals are struggling to maintain adequate health services for their communities. A national need exists to provide graduate training in public

health and health administration to these vital institutions of our national infrastructure. A promising mechanism is the use of graduate courses delivered online to students in isolated areas and to other students whose work and family commitments keep them from attending classes at a university.

For academic institutions that wish to meet this societal need, *Online Education: 6 Steps to Starting an Online School* offers "how-to" instructions and advice based on the author's extensive experience in developing a successful online school with master's degrees in public health, health administration, and geriatric health management. The book also serves as an excellent guide for colleges and universities considering online programs in other disciplines.

The well-written narrative provides real-life examples to illustrate the general principles of academic program development and administration. This pioneering work is a useful reference in the evolution of distance graduate education and recommended reading for those who wish to advance this application of technology to graduate education. I hope you find it as engaging and helpful as I did.

Michael E. Samuels, Dr.P.H.

Distinguished Scholar and Endowed Chair in Rural Health Policy

Professor of Family Practice and Community Medicine
University of Kentucky College of Medicine

FOREWORD

This process-oriented book presents the what-to-do and how-to-do-it methods for starting an online graduate school within an existing institution of higher learning. The focus is on a school with two or more programs at the master's level, but the book's material on planning and development can be applied to online schools that have programs at any or all degree levels. The book is written from the point of view of its author. It makes no attempt to compare or contrast other methods, and no attempt to assess the pros or cons of various other e-learning software. The author also does not evaluate the many successes of alternative strategies.

The principles and concepts that guide the author's process are familiar to any academic who has been involved in course or program development. The principal key to the success of process is in the planning—planning well in advance of need to ensure the resources required for forward motion are in place and systems are operational. The well-disciplined, future-thinking manager will find the six steps to starting an online school easy to understand.

Each of the book's six chapters discusses an area that must be addressed in the planning, development, and implementation of an online school. The discussions reflect the perspective of someone who actually went through the process, from concept to reality. The school the author started accepted its first students in December 1999. By February 2005, with over

430 online students from all over the U.S. and several foreign countries, the school had a surplus—revenues less operational expenses—of over $200,000.

Some discussions are brief factual accounts of how the author accomplished a task. Other topics are examined in greater depth, often including observations derived from the author's personal experiences in dealing with the obstacles and pitfalls he encountered.

The appendix contains three supplemental chapters (Appendices C, D, and E) about the three master's degree programs implemented at the author's school—public health, health administration, and geriatric health management— from a process perspective. Although the three chapters speak to specific degree programs, the application of the process discussed provides guidance to program developers in any discipline.

This book is written for the person needing a short guide covering the topics pertinent to the success of the endeavor. As you read, feel free to contact the author with your own experiences, contrasting methods, or topics you feel have been left out or not fully addressed.

1.
Curriculum

Mission Statements as the Basis for Planning

Curriculum planning is a critical element of the overall planning process. The starting point for planning a curriculum is your university's *institutional mission statement*. The institutional mission serves as the foundation for the development of a mission statement for a school within the university, and both the institution's and the school's mission statements serve as the foundation for the development of a program's mission statement.

The *program mission* reflects the institutional and school missions while stating a purpose or goal specific to the program. A program mission, then, includes a restatement of those parts of the institutional and school missions that relate to the individual program, while setting forth the purpose or primary goal of the program. End the mission statement by citing your program's commitment to integrity and excellence. To further define your program, you can augment the statement with a list of goals, objectives, and values with regard to students, faculty, and staff. But the mission statement itself should be short.

Curriculum planning flows from the program's mission statement. The courses, training opportunities, and other aspects of the curriculum are developed with an eye toward

achieving the stated mission. If the curriculum does not support the mission, your institution will not meet the needs of your students. It will also have difficulty qualifying for any specialized accreditation, and it may encounter problems with your institution's regional accreditor. In designing a curriculum, keep in mind that each course and its content must contribute in some way to the program's success in meeting its mission statement.

Credit Hours

Determining the total credits hours required for program completion is an important decision, one that takes several factors into account. Begin by learning about other similar programs. Use the Internet to review their curricula. What courses and credits do the other programs offer, particularly those programs at well-regarded institutions that attract the best students? Once you know what others are doing, you can make a decision on the courses and credits you will offer. If possible, create a program that is the "shortest time to degree." By being the shortest, in terms of total credit hours, your program will have an added market appeal. Many prospective students will be attracted to your program because it allows them to complete their degree or certificate requirements sooner than their peers in similar programs offered by other schools. By being the shortest, your program will also be less expensive, since tuition is calculated per credit hour. If you offer multiple degrees, keep all total credit requirements for all degrees the same. Plan an equal number of courses for each discipline. This will make it easier to track students and keep records, and to schedule the courses.

The determination of the number of credit hours given to an online course is a decision made by each offering institution.

No hard rules for credit-per-course determinations exist. Even today, with online education offered by most public universities and a growing number of private universities, and even some secondary schools, this decision is entirely yours. The generally accepted rule is: One quarter hour credit is worth about two-thirds of a semester hour credit. A ten-week quarter would result in three quarter hours of credit per course. You may decide on a different formula, but be prepared to defend your decision if asked by accrediting agencies or competing institutions. The conversion of "online time" to "seat time" considers the reading of assignments, note taking from online presentations, synchronous weekly chat sessions, asynchronous participations in threaded-discussion forums, any group work or special assignments by the instructor, and the time spent taking online quizzes and exams. These should equal about four hours of seat time weekly for a course with three quarter credits.

Using semester credits, however, is preferable to using quarter credits. Semester credits are more common in higher education, so most students have an understanding of them. Converting seat time to credits is simplified, and you will not need to defend the use of quarter credits if your institution otherwise awards semester credits. If you want to do something different, consider offering a year-round program by breaking a one-year period into trimesters, with each trimester equivalent to one semester in terms of total seat time.

Course Sequencing and Coding

Assigning identifying letters and numbers to the courses you offer should conform to your institution's style or the style customary in higher education. Course numbering should reflect the level at which courses are offered. Generally,

3

undergraduate courses use 100-500, except that senior-level or focus courses sometimes use 600; graduate courses use 700-900; professional-level courses use 1,000 and above.

Also assign each course three letters. The three letters indicate the program affiliation. For example, "MPH 735" could be used to indicate a graduate course in a Master of Public Health program. Core courses, or courses common to two or more programs, have the same numbers, but the courses are listed under each program with the letters identifying that program. You might also consider sequencing the numbers to correspond with the program to which the course belongs. For example, the 700-750 level could be core courses, the 800 series public health, and the 900 series another discipline.

Avoid tight sequencing when assigning course numbers. You will want to add courses as your program evolves, and you will need a spread in the numbering so the new courses can be inserted in the proper sequence without changing the numbers of existing courses. At the beginning, provide ten numbers between each course just for this reason.

Using Core Courses to "Jump Start" All Programs

Course selection is key to the eventual success of new online educational programs. By creating core courses that will fit well into the curricula of two or more of the programs you intend to offer, you can "jump start" total registrations while keeping costs to a minimum.

A core course is one that provides basic, foundational content appropriate for more than one discipline. If three to five core courses are common to the curricula of all your programs, then you can start offering courses by having all students, regardless of the programs in which they enroll, take the same core courses. You will be able to register many students in

different programs at relatively little cost. If you decide, for instance, to create three programs with 12 courses each, five of which are core courses common to all three programs, you could recruit for all three programs and have only the five core courses to develop initially. By using the *Just-in-Time* (JIT) model, a term borrowed from manufacturing to describe the process of having raw materials delivered to a plant just in time for their use, you can develop courses incrementally. You will be able to register students in each program without spending additional money creating program-specific courses that initially would have few registrants. Over time, all courses will fill, and you will need to offer extra sections of the courses.

Tracking Course Content

A *content matrix* is a tool for tracking the content of courses and to facilitate the changing or updating of course content. It is a simple spreadsheet that lists courses across the top and content items down the left side (see Appendix A).

A content matrix serves several purposes. It gives you a visual representation of where content is being offered, showing you how many times the same content appears in the curriculum. It will enable you to see where content is missing or unnecessarily repeated, and where content might be moved to better meet students' needs. A content matrix, if created using content recommendations from accrediting bodies, both regional and specialized, will guarantee your curriculum contains all content necessary to meet requirements.

The Course Rollout: A Long-Range Course Schedule

The *course rollout*, or the course schedule, has an important role in the planning process. The course rollout should cover the first five to seven years. Scheduling courses this far in

advance may seem unnecessary, and it is not an easy task, but you will need a firm long-term course schedule for planning your courses well ahead of time. The course rollout contains the following:

Course letters and number;

Course name;

Faculty person;

FACE (faculty assistant course expert, discussed in chapter 2);

Number of credits;

Term start date (start on a Monday);

Any holiday or break dates;

Term end date (end on a Friday); and

Final grade due date (see Appendix B).

By planning for multiple rollout years, you will also be assured of having your courses listed in the master university calendar and catalog. The rollout, if done properly and accurately, will prove a valuable tool. You will refer to it often in planning your programs.

Conferring Both Degrees and Certificates

Your program should offer both degrees and certificates. A certificate is typically two-thirds of a degree. It is offered to those students who are not convinced they need a degree but would like evidence of academic credit in a particular field, either for a job promotion or a new job. Certificate credit is no different than degree credit. Those courses that certificate students take are the same ones degree students take, taught by the same faculty. The level of course completion and mastery of course content is identical to the level required of degree students, and certificate credits should count toward degrees for students who may decide later to seek degrees. Certificate

students should be expected to meet the same admission requirements as degree students.

Being flexible to student needs will help increase enrollments. Many adult online students do not want or cannot make the commitment to a degree, but they have a need for a certificate. Most of these students, however, will go on to complete the degree requirements if they can count their certificate credits toward the degree requirements. Additionally, the U.S. military often provides tuition assistance for certificate programs, but not degree programs. Students who complete certificate programs with military assistance can later take the additional courses required for a degree, using other tuition assistance or their own funds.

Three sections at the end of this book—Appendices C, D, and E—are first-person accounts of the process used for the design and development of three online graduate programs at the author's school. The programs offer certificates and master's degrees in public health, health administration, and geriatric health management. The appendices are complementary material for review following your reading of the book's six chapters.

2.

Courses

A Systemized Process for Course Planning and Development

Using a systemized process for course planning will enable you to create courses with standardized formats, while ensuring that content throughout your programs' curricula is comprehensive and non-repetitive.

Decide early in the process whether to have prerequisites in your curricula. Designating certain courses within a curriculum as required for subsequent courses is not always necessary. If subject material in one course requires a thorough knowledge of material covered in another course, then that course should definitely be a prerequisite. If possible, though, plan your online programs' curricula so students may take courses in any sequence. You might still recommend that students take certain courses before taking others, but not requiring that they do so will greatly facilitate course scheduling later. Course sequencing with prerequisites can become complicated as the numbers of registered students, degrees, and courses increase. Keeping things simple is the best way to proceed.

The one exception with regard to avoiding prerequisites is that all new students should take the same first course, which would be a core course common to the curricula of all your online programs. In this way, you can create an orientation session for the new students that includes a preview of the first

course they will be taking. Including the course preview will better prepare those students for whom your programs will be their first experience in online education.

In planning the curriculum, list the courses in some logical sequence. If one course is a prerequisite for another, then the sequencing of those courses is important and can be suggested by the numbers designated for the courses. But, again, avoid prerequisites if possible.

Course design and development should follow an established format, which is mostly determined by the e-learning software you will use. The better-known software programs incorporate the elements found in typical online courses, such as textual materials, forums or threaded discussions, chat sessions, and audio-visual presentations. Online courses also make use of quizzes, exams, student papers, and student presentations, and these elements, too, are standard components of most e-learning software.

The content of a specific course flows from and is the responsibility of the instructor and the faculty assistant course expert (FACE), a staff member who is part educator and part information technology specialist. The process by which the instructor and the FACE incorporate the courses goals, objectives, and outcomes also influences course content. An instructor should approach the course with an outline of the content, using the content matrix as a guide, and dividing the course into units that correspond to weeks, a set number of textbook chapters, or specific topics related to the overall subject matter. Units usually are segmented into a set number of weeks and structured according to the chapter sequence of the textbook, but a different order for the units, one that skips back and forth in the textbook, or a different basis for the units

can be used if it lends itself to better teaching of the course's content.

From the unit outline, the instructor creates the specific tasks required to accomplish the unit's goal. Each unit should have a goal-and-objectives statement, not only as a guide for constructing the course, but also to establish each unit's learning expectations of students. Task elements can include textual materials, such as *lectures* and *notes*, which are created with Microsoft Word. Lectures should be relatively short—readings that take from ten to 20 minutes—and should explain or clarify materials found in textbooks and assignments. Notes should explain difficult concepts and include examples of them.

Using *forums*, or threaded discussions, is an excellent way to generate online interchange among students. This asynchronous, or "not-at-the-same-time," tool permits students to respond to questions or comments at any time. Students, no matter when they access the discussion, can see the questions and comments by the earlier participants in the forum. Throughout the duration of a course's unit, the instructor can offer guidance if the students stray from the topic.

Audio-visual presentations are well suited for teaching difficult material online. Using a PowerPoint presentation with audio overlay can be very effective in explaining concepts and principles. But faculty members need to do more than simply read the presentation's textual slides; they must enlarge upon the text, adding to its meaning by providing examples that illustrate the points being presented.

Audio is created using the Sound Recorder feature of a personal computer's operating system. A transcription of the audio portion of a presentation must be posted online to meet the guidelines of the Americans with Disabilities Act.

Allow online access to the transcription for all students in the course.

Using *chat sessions* in the form of "office hours" gives students opportunities to interact with their instructors and one another. Chat sessions are synchronous, meaning "at the same time" or "in real time." They enable live interactions. Any scheduled session, however, will almost always be inconvenient for some students. The best way to schedule chat sessions is to set the first session in advance and then have everyone participate in setting the dates and times for future sessions.

Chat sessions should be structured, usually in the form of an agenda prepared by the instructor, to ensure the time is well spent. Encourage students who cannot participate in a session to e-mail questions or comments ahead of time. Each session can be archived, making it available to the students who could not participate. Later, they can view the session to see how their questions or comments were addressed. Each unit of a course should have "office hour" chat sessions.

Online courses sometimes use *video presentations*, but they can detract from the quality of online educational programs, even when students have high-speed Internet connections. If you would like to use video, try to keep it limited to short introductions of material or topics, and keep the bandwidth requirements low and the time short, no more than 30 seconds. For many students, nothing is more boring than a "talking head" on a computer screen.

The development process for each course, then, is one of breaking the course into manageable pieces. Work on the units as they come, and complete all tasks in each unit before moving on to the next one. The FACE will translate the content into HTML format or to PowerPoint and audio formats compatible with the e-learning software. All material for a course and all

tasks associated with it must be completed before the course begins. Do not allow instructors to create content "on the fly." It rarely works, and it creates anxiety for staff, students, and the instructors themselves. Finishing the course material and related tasks at least three weeks before the start date also allows time for administrative review and final editing.

Intellectual Property Issues

Issues related to faculty intellectual property always come up during the development of courses. Online program instructors generally work as independent contractors, hired for a relatively brief period to perform a specific job, a "work made for hire." Your instructors will want to offer their very best efforts to your online courses, and they will want to include in the courses material that they previously developed themselves, which is their intellectual property. Encourage your instructors, then, to incorporate into their courses any related supplemental materials they have authored.

The institution's intellectual property encompasses the software used for online programs, the institution's infrastructure, and its support services, including the administrative, curricular, and financial support provided the instructor. The extensive use of the institution's intellectual property, along with the "work-made-for-hire" contract, is the reason course ownership belongs to the institution. Course ownership is highly important for financial reasons. Your institution will not want to pay future royalties to an instructor who may not even be by then on contract with the institution.

The Role of the Faculty Assistant Course Expert

Qualified technical support is essential during the

development of an online course. Technical support is provided by FACEs, the faculty assistant course experts. FACEs serve as translators, taking instructors' content and preparing it for delivery to students, making it easy for them to access and understand.

FACEs are typically information technology specialists with experience in education, personnel trained in Web site development who know how to make full use of the software selected for the job. But FACEs are not only technicians but administrators as well, keeping instructors on schedule and making sure the courses are constructed and presented so as to accomplish their goals and objectives. FACEs do not determine content, but they do advise instructors on ways to present the content. FACEs suggest the best methods and formats for presenting material, joining the instructor in critiquing the results.

Initially, a FACE functions as a technical assistant to lead faculty persons—those instructors who create new courses—by converting their lectures and course materials to Web formats, transcribing audio files, and preparing PowerPoint slides. The FACE keeps lead faculty persons on schedule in creating new courses, without making them feel rushed or stressed. One way FACEs can manage lead faculty persons is by establishing a production schedule for them to follow. The schedule gives the instructors ample time for their duties at their home institutions while creating a course for one of your online programs. Nine months is the norm for creating a course, not including the time it takes to recruit the faculty person. But once the lead faculty person is under contract, the nine-month period should suffice for covering all steps in the course-creation process, from an initial draft of the course goals and objectives through final editing and review. During the course-creation phase, the

FACE manages the production schedule. Appendix C has a list of the major items included in a production schedule.

After courses have started and until the term ends, the FACE supports instructors by sending reminders of assignments, tracking assignment deadlines, and forwarding the completed student assignments to instructors. Because e-mails do occasionally disappear into cyberspace, the FACE keeps a copy of all material forwarded from students to instructors. The FACE, and the instructors as well, should also keep copies of correspondence and tests. To help instructors and students with technical problems they may encounter, the FACE attends the first few chat sessions of every course section, every term. The FACE also performs minor editing duties and repairs any broken links that occur. In brief, a FACE does the "work" of the course, serving administrators, instructors, and students.

Each course being offered during a term, and each section of the course, has an assigned FACE. The number of FACEs your programs need will increase as the number of your courses increases. One FACE with a high level of expertise on your e-learning software can work simultaneously with lead faculty persons in developing three or four new courses, while managing three or four established courses. During periods when no new courses are in development, an experienced FACE can simultaneously manage nine or ten established courses. The FACE assigned to the first course that all new students take, however, usually has responsibilities for only this one core course and all its sections. All FACEs participate in annual work sessions with instructors to update and maintain the content of courses.

Finding the right person to fill a FACE position will probably not be easy. You will need someone with advanced technical skills—an information technology specialist—who

also has a background in education. The author has been successful in recruiting qualified FACEs from among retired high school teachers—individuals still desiring to work, still highly motivated, but no longer interested in teaching at the high-school level. After a period of orientation on campus, FACEs can work online from their homes, which they find appealing. The job is also attractive in that it allows for creativity in devising online instructional presentations. As a FACE, a former teacher can continue to make meaningful contributions to the field of education while doing challenging and rewarding work.

Your school's administration will support the course-development process by providing the personnel, resources, guidance, and students. The administration should do everything possible to make course development easy for the instructor. Finally, the administration should be respectful of instructors by offering them fair contracts and ongoing support as courses are developed and taught.

A Uniform Structure for All Courses

Course structure should be consistent, with all courses having the same structural elements located in the same places as the courses progress. Students look for the structural elements within a course, expecting to find them consistently placed and in the same formats from course to course. Structural consistency among all courses helps prevent student anxiety and reduces questions.

Course materials include information on the course's structure. These materials inform students of what lies ahead. They tell students the requirements for successful completion of the course.

Begin with a course *syllabus*. The syllabus sets forth the

unit divisions, assignments by date, the dates for quizzes and exams, and any breaks in the schedule. Deadlines for readings and assignments should also be in the syllabus. Placing this information in a column format and color coding the various elements make a syllabus easy for students to follow.

Once the syllabus is completed, applying the information it contains to a *calendar* is easy. Most e-learning software has an interactive, or hyperlinked, calendar. Clicking on a hyperlink in the calendar takes the student to the task. The calendar for each student can be individualized, allowing students to use their course calendars for entering their personal appointments and reminder notes.

Another structural element of great importance is *grading*. In describing how students will be graded, be sure instructors include the grade scale, the items that will be graded, and the method the instructor will use in grading exams, quizzes, papers, and other assignments.

For example, if the assignment is to write a paper, a student should know the total available points that can be earned for the paper. Of those points, a student should also know the number assigned to content, grammar, style, format, and consistency. In other words, an instructor informs students of the criteria used in grading an assignment and how the total available points will be distributed over those criteria. Then the instructor sticks to that grading method. Instructors may not say they are going to grade something one way and then grade it another. The administration, if a student complains, could not defend an instructor who departed from a course's published grading method.

Instruments for Evaluating Student Learning

Evaluation tools deserve a separate discussion. *Objective*

tests are in one way well suited for online educational programs. Students receive immediate feedback on their performance, the moment they submit the test. But objective tests—those using multiple-choice, true-false, matching, and short-answer questions—should not be the sole evaluation instrument used. Instructors must also consider assigning *individual* and *group papers*. A student-written paper allows an instructor to evaluate not only learning, but thought process and expression as well. Group paper assignments allow several students to collaborate, each producing a portion of the paper, but all sharing in the grade. Group-work online simulates cooperative group-work found in business and the professions. Individual and group papers should be three or four pages in length and conform to a commonly accepted style, such as the rules and guidelines in the *Publication Manual of the American Psychological Association.*

When grading a paper, an instructor can mark it up using the "tracking" feature in Microsoft Word. The tracking feature lets an instructor enter corrections, comments, and suggestions—all the things instructors like to do on papers. The instructor can electronically return the paper and let the student use the corrections, comments, and suggestions in resubmitting it.

E-mail is another avenue for assessing student learning. An instructor can evaluate a student by the level of understanding a student's e-mail messages reflect and the kinds of questions the student asks.

Having *phone conversations* with students is another way for instructors to evaluate student learning. Similarly, *chat sessions* yield a lot of information about how a student thinks and responds in a spontaneous setting. They too can be used as an evaluation tool.

Whatever evaluation instruments the instructor uses,

students must be aware of them. In the syllabus or another course document, an instructor needs to inform the students of all the ways their learning will be assessed, including the criteria used in the assessments.

Creating a Capstone Appropriate for Online Education

An educational program's culminating event, called a "capstone," demonstrates the extent to which a student has mastered the program's material. It encompasses the student's total learning experience while enrolled in the program. Institutional accrediting agencies and many specialized accrediting agencies require capstones.

A capstone is typically a comprehensive term paper at the bachelor's level, a thesis or original research project at the master's level, and a dissertation incorporating original research at the doctoral level. Online educational programs can require these same capstones, but you may choose to create a different kind of capstone, one less likely to garner the fear that a required thesis or dissertation often provokes. Less intimidating would be a capstone project completed incrementally as the student progresses through the various courses. A capstone assignment incorporated into each course would fulfill a requirement of the course and become part of the final capstone as well.

For each course, then, a capstone project could be constructed to meet one of the course objectives, serving as an evaluation tool for the instructor while also contributing to a larger project. The larger project, when completed, would contain the individual course capstone assignments and a summary paper that would bring all aspects of a student's educational experience together. The summary paper could incorporate a SWOT analysis. SWOT analyses—which consider a product's "Strengths, Weaknesses, Opportunities,

and Threats"—are marketing assessments used in the business world. They can also be applied in education. Using incremental capstone assignments and a summary paper to complete the final capstone would satisfy the requirements of institutional and specialized accreditors.

Institutional and Specialized Accrediting Agencies

Accreditation is one of the more significant driving forces behind course and curriculum development. Accreditation requirements influence the curriculum content and the frequency that specific content is offered. Accreditation also drives evaluation processes and many of the postgraduate activities.

Higher education accrediting agencies are of two basic kinds. Institutional accreditors include the six regional accrediting agencies recognized by the U.S. Secretary of Education. Far outnumbering the institutional accreditors are the many specialized accrediting agencies, also known as programmatic accrediting agencies. The Secretary of Education recognizes about 50 specialized agencies, but many others exist. Several of these other specialized agencies have demonstrated their reliability by obtaining recognition from the Council for Higher Education Accreditation.

The word "accreditation" as generally used refers to the institutional accreditation granted by one of the six regional accreditors. All six have agreed on a single set of requirements for the online educational programs offered by their accredited institutions. All regionally accredited colleges and universities, then, wherever they are located, must meet the same standards in offering online programs.

Specialized or programmatic accrediting agencies accredit individual schools and programs within larger institutions.

Where the entire institution consists of a single program, such as a freestanding professional school, the specialized accreditor for that profession may act as the institutional accreditor, especially if the school does not have regional accreditation.

Specialized accreditation of your institution, school, or program can present problems when it comes to offering online courses. A specialized accreditor may say it does not discriminate against online programs, but the agency's requirements, if geared only for campus-based programs, will make online offerings difficult or even impossible. Typically, a specialized agency has standards that include full-time faculty requirements, space requirements, original research requirements, and comprehensive student services requirements. The time and resources required to meet the standards can be prohibitive for online programs. Some specialized agencies, however, do have appropriate standards for online programs. Depending on your situation, you may want to consider establishing your online programs outside the purview of any specialized accreditor but still under the mantle of your institution's regional accreditation.

Before starting work on the development of an online program, check with your institutional accreditor, as well as with your specialized accreditor if applicable, to see if it requires advance notice of new instructional or delivery methods. Most accreditors do, and most also require advance notice of new degree and certificate programs. So if your degree programs and certificate are new, you will probably need to submit detailed information as much as nine months in advance. Become highly knowledgeable of your institutional accreditor's standards for online programs, and your specialized accreditor's if applicable. The requirements of the standards will greatly affect course development and curriculum planning.

The online degree programs that the author created were in areas where specialized accreditation was available but, because the specialized accreditors had developed their standards for campus-based programs, they were not appropriate for online programs. The author therefore chose not to seek specialized accreditation.

Library Privileges for Online Students

Student use of outside information resources is as important in online programs as it is in campus-based programs. Your institution's library should offer your online students Internet access to the appropriate journals and other information resources. Take an active role on the library committee, lobbying for the resources your students will need. As you develop your online programs, work with your institution's information technology (IT) department to ensure student access to your institution's library and other online libraries.

The experiences of other administrators in online education have shown that an institution's IT department can either facilitate or hinder access to library holdings by online students. Gain the cooperation of IT personnel early on. From the beginning, share your plans with them and seek their advice. Your life will be much easier.

First, a Course Orientation Session

An effective course orientation session inspires students to make their best efforts in succeeding. Do not underestimate its value. Require the session for every new student to your online offerings. Using a live webcast service enables a high degree of interaction. Students can ask questions, learn how to use the buttons and links, and preview the first week's assignments. The session is conducted by a FACE and student adviser.

The session covers all the buttons and links, the syllabus, the interactive calendar, assignment due dates, and the grading method. Include a sample PowerPoint presentation with audio. The orientation should also cover administrative processes and your institution's policies on cheating, plagiarism, academic probation, and dismissal. At the author's school, all first-time students took the same core course, and the orientation session was exactly the same for all new students regardless of the programs in which they were enrolled. The session included a preview of the course, with student access to the course, and guided instruction to hyperlinks, tabs, the syllabus, and other content items.

Three Kinds of Courses: Core, Program Specific, and Focus

Core courses—those foundational courses that are shared by two or more of your programs—have already been discussed. Again, they are critically important for the early success of your program. By initially offering only the core courses common to all your online degree and certificate programs, you can simultaneously enroll students in multiple disciplines at minimal cost. This approach generates the revenue needed for developing and implementing the later courses, and it gives each of your programs a student base from which to grow.

Program-specific courses are those courses required for a particular degree or certificate, in addition to the required core courses. Your Internet search of online programs similar to your own as offered at other institutions helps you in determining the program-specific courses you will offer. Develop them as needed, but begin work far enough in advance so the courses will be ready when students complete the core courses. Using the Just-in-Time model is a way to pace your expenditures by creating courses as they are needed.

Focus courses concentrate on a challenging aspect of a particular subject, a narrow topic of special importance, or a research project. Focus courses are often offered as "concentrations" with partnership institutions, discussed later.

Writing Course Descriptions

For all courses, prepare *course descriptions* for publication in the catalog. The description of each course should reflect the program mission, with the content matrix serving as your guide for writing a brief statement of course goals and objectives.

Course descriptions also include a statement of course outcomes, or the ways a course will benefit students—what the course is expected to accomplish for students and, thus, what students are expected to accomplish in the course. Later, the stated outcomes will serve as the basis for developing ways to measure student achievement. The measurement of student achievement, using instruments that could range from quizzes to student-produced online PowerPoint presentations, is a major emphasis of accrediting agencies.

A Three-Phase Process for Evaluating Courses

Course evaluations are a necessity for the ongoing improvement of your programs. The evaluation of each course each time it is offered, and each of its sections, is conducted in three phases.

The first phase is an evaluation by the students in the course. Create an evaluation form for online delivery to all students in each course during the last week of the term. Require students to complete the form. Most e-learning software has a feature that will allow blocking of other functions if the form is not submitted by its due date. The evaluation form queries students on topics related to course content and the instructor.

It also covers the delivery technology, download times, the quality of the online slide and audio presentations, and ways to improve the course.

The second phase of the evaluation process focuses on the instructor's skills as an online educator. The evaluation is prepared by the FACE and covers the instructor's promptness in meeting student needs, e-mail reply times, forum discussion participation, and other aspects of the instructor's performance that the FACE observed. The FACE does not evaluate content.

Content, however, *is* evaluated by the program director in the third phase of the evaluation process. The program director assesses the extent to which the content taught met the course goals and objectives, and whether the stated outcomes were actually accomplished. The program director also evaluates the effectiveness of the instructor's teaching methods in light of the same criteria.

The three phases of the course evaluation are summarized in a report that the academic dean uses as a basis for approving or rejecting the instructor for additional contracts. A copy of the report is sent to the instructor soon after the completion of the course, no more than 30 days later. If the instructor has been approved for future contracts, the dean notes this in the cover letter. If the dean did not approve the instructor for future contracts, the cover letter only needs to thank the instructor for teaching the course. Because all contracts are one-time contracts, no instructor is ever really fired. Those few instructors who may not meet expectations are simply not offered future contracts.

Posting Course Information on Your Web Site

The public *Web site* for your online programs is your main tool for communicating with prospective and current students.

Post on the Web site all the information you want them to have, keeping in mind their needs. Among the items you should post are:

1. *A general syllabus for every course offered.* A general syllabus is absent dates so it will have "shelf life." It includes information about course activities and assignments, giving prospective students an indication of the time they will need to devote to the course. The information helps them decide when to take the course in view of other demands on their time.

2. *Your course calendar.* The course calendar covers current and future years. It shows the courses that will be offered in each term. Unless you will be doing the extraordinary by offering every course in every term, the course calendar is an essential part of your Web site. It tells students when a particular course is available so they can plan their schedules.

3. *An academic calendar.* The calendar lists critical due dates and deadlines. Students desire information well in advance to make decisions. Typically, three or four years' worth of dates are listed.

4. *Course surveys.* Reviews of each course are prepared following completion of the course evaluations. Ideally, the surveys include comments of previous students or other excerpts from the course evaluations. Course surveys help prospective students of a course to decide when to take it in light of their schedules and the different instructors who teach the course from term to term.

Your public Web site is a highly cost-effective means of keeping current students fully informed and recruiting new students. In every way it must reflect the vitality and professionalism of your programs.

3.

Faculty

Program Directors: Uncommon Individuals

At the very beginning of the faculty-development phase for your online school, your major concern will be to identify a *program director* (PD) for each of your online programs. The first part of the selection process is to list possible candidates teaching at well-known universities and colleges, individuals who have academic credentials at the doctoral level, are extensively published, and are well regarded in their fields. It is desirable, too, that they have a complementary credential in business, education, or leadership. These individuals are uncommon, but they will bring a wealth of experience and a large network of influence with them. Limit your recruiting efforts to those who meet these criteria. Their expertise and active involvement in their fields will contribute significantly to your programs' ongoing improvement by opening avenues for innovation and exchange.

PDs are hired as part-time employees. As persons directing others and responsible for decisions, employment laws normally require that they be employees, not independent contractors. PDs complete a W-4 form, and regulations regarding federal and state payroll withholdings apply. You want PDs to be part time so they can maintain their home affiliations and home networks. You do not need to incur the expense of hiring

them full time, because your other employees can carry out the related day-to-day activities.

As of this book's publication, a part-time annual salary of $15,000 for PDs is the generally accepted norm. The salary is paid in equal monthly amounts. Your PD contract, however, is made more attractive by adding incentives for bringing students into the program. Specify in the contract that a *one-time* incentive will be paid whenever a *first-time* student registers for the initial core course if the student would not have registered *but for* the program director. The italicized words are important. They make clear that an incentive is paid only when the PD's efforts are responsible for a new student's registration, and that the same student's later registration in any additional courses does not qualify for additional incentive pay. The contract includes the amount of the incentive, perhaps about ten percent of the tuition for the initial core course. Incentive pay is treated the same as employee earnings, with applicable deductions each month.

Incentives can only help in building your program. For the PDs, incentives are compensation well earned for their efforts in sharing information about your program with others who could benefit from it.

A PD is responsible for designing the program's curriculum; finalizing the course titles, descriptions, goals, objectives, and outcomes; and ensuring that the content matrix is followed, which is important for accreditation purposes. A PD will have a lot of work initially, but over time the workload will lighten. The monthly salary and any incentives as time goes on will compensate for the relatively heavy workload at first.

Ask prospective PDs to obtain clearance from their home institutions for their part-time work with your institution. Some private universities prohibit their faculty members from

working for other institutions, but public universities generally do not. Being open about your school's engagement of PDs, as well as instructors and any consultants you may hire, prevents public relations problems in the future.

To build and maintain relationships and to be a working team member, PDs must be available for phone calls, e-mail exchanges, live webcasts, and in-person job performance at your institution at least quarterly. Your program covers the expenses for their travel.

Value your PDs. They will add immeasurably to the academic excellence of your online programs, ensuring their success. You will find they are dedicated people who truly want to provide students the best in the way of educational programs. If you are able to pay your PDs above the recommendation, do so. But PDs do this work not for the money but because they enjoy sharing their time and experience with others who are also committed to high quality in educational programs.

Lead Faculty: Instructors Who Create Your Courses

Lead faculty persons are the special people who place their professional reputations at risk by undertaking the creation of a new course for online delivery. Make sure they receive all the help they need from the FACE and your institution's other faculty support services.

As of this book's publication, the generally accepted norm for lead faculty compensation is $3,000. For someone charged with the hard work of developing a new course, a nine-month project in itself, and then teaching the course the first time it is offered, $3,000 is not a great deal of money. But lead faculty instructors know that a successful course, one that remains in the curriculum for years to come, will in the future be less demanding on their time and energies. Instructors receive the

fee, which may increase over the years, each additional time they teach the course.

Lead faculty persons develop their new courses according to the specifications required by the content matrix. They will likely expect to be well compensated for their time, hard work, professional expertise, and the use of their intellectual property, so be prepared to explain that the $3,000 fee will be there again and again, each time the instructor teaches the course. Over time, your lead faculty persons will be well compensated for their contributions.

Adjunct Faculty: Instructors for Your "Cloned Courses"

Adjunct faculty persons are the instructors who teach the courses already in place, the courses created by lead faculty. Management, content, and quality-control issues would emerge if newly contracted faculty persons were to create their own versions of courses already in the curriculum, courses that have demonstrated their effectiveness as originally designed.

Because the courses that adjunct faculty teach are courses that have already been offered at least once and probably several times by lead faculty, the assurance exists that their content is sound and adheres to curriculum and accreditation requirements. These "cloned courses" are exact replications of the courses that lead faculty developed, taught in exactly the same way. Cloned courses do not infringe upon the academic freedom of adjunct faculty. The principles of academic freedom extend to an instructor's unique style of interacting with students, but not to the course content, its format, or the order of presentation. Bypass prospective instructors who do not want to teach "someone else's course." It will not be difficult to find instructors who would be pleased to have the opportunity.

Hiring Instructors as Independent Contractors

Unless a compelling reason exists for hiring instructors full time, such as an institutional rule or policy, the more cost-effective way is to hire them part time as *independent contractors*. Most of your instructors will prefer this arrangement because it allows them to remain affiliated with their home institutions.

The U.S. Department of Labor and the Internal Revenue Service have guidelines for determining whether someone is legally an employee or a contractor, regardless of designations as they may appear in any written agreements. State labor departments generally publish guidelines as well, based on the federal guidelines and court rulings. But an individual does not need to meet all the federal and state guidelines to qualify legally as an independent contractor. Generally, anyone who has or recently has had other contracts, or anyone who is employed by someone else, can easily qualify as an independent contractor for a short-term, specific assignment. Nevertheless, use the Internet to become knowledgeable of the federal and state guidelines that pertain to employee-versus-contractor status. The knowledge will assure you of the appropriateness of your hiring practices and enable you to address concerns others may raise.

Additional sections of a course are simultaneously offered whenever the number of course registrants requires them. A section has a set number of students, from 20 to 30, depending on the subject matter of the course. For the more difficult courses that require more teaching time, sections have fewer students than the sections for the less demanding courses. The number of students that constitute a course's section is an administrative decision, not a faculty decision. A statement to this effect should appear in your faculty handbook. Adjunct

faculty persons are paid per section at one-half the rate for lead faculty.

Identifying and Recruiting Qualified Instructors

Identifying prospective instructors begins with a review of the qualifications of your institution's current faculty members. You will be looking for those who have the appropriate credentials for teaching online courses in your programs' disciplines. Begin with the faculty members who teach courses in the same disciplines as your online programs. Review their education, verify their degrees, and review their course evaluations. If you are starting a new degree program with courses not already taught on campus, it is unlikely any current faculty members at all will be qualified, although some may try to convince you otherwise.

Set your goals for faculty high. If you cannot find instructors who fully meet your standards from among your institution's own ranks, then expand your search by reviewing textbooks in your programs' disciplines. For each program, contact the authors whose books most closely match your curricular objectives and the content matrix you have created. You will be pleasantly surprised by how many authors, even the well-known ones who "wrote the book" on a particular subject, will be interested in working for your school. They may never have taught an online course, but they have wanted to for a long time and would welcome the experience. Tell them how your FACE can help them. Once recruited, many of these well-regarded authorities will remain active instructors for years to come.

You might also find some possible future instructors teaching at other colleges and universities in your area. Check the Web sites for those institutions or obtain their catalogs.

The catalogs are probably available at the local public library and your institution's library.

Information on the Internet is yet another way to identify prospects. Search for "online education" or visit the Web site for eInstructors.Inc (www.eInstructors.Com). eInstructors. Inc makes referrals to faculty persons interested in teaching online.

After you have developed a list of possible instructors and learned as much as you could about each one's qualifications, select the people you would most like to have. Contact them directly and pose the question, a simple question, one that works quite often: "Would you be interested in teaching online?"

Once your online program is operational, your program directors become your best resource for recruiting replacement and additional instructors. Each PD has a lifetime of contacts in higher education. Begin with having your PDs teach at least one course. Your objective here is to give them firsthand experience so they will have an expert's understanding of the process. Their experience will enable them to answer all the questions prospective instructors ask. Plus, the enthusiasm of the PDs, bolstered by their personal involvement in online education, will make a highly positive impression on the prospective instructors they contact.

Using online recruiting services is the most effective way to expand your faculty when registrations begin to surge. This increased need for more instructors usually develops in the fourth or fifth year of operation. By this time, courses will have been taught several times, and lead faculty persons will have refined them with respect to format, flow, and results.

Recruiting faculty by using online recruiting and referral services begins with identifying those firms that provide value-added services. One firm that offers value-add referral

services is eInstructors.Com. "Value added" as used here means the credentials of prospective faculty members have already been verified. Advertisements seeking new faculty members will bring many applications, but verifying that an applicant is really the person the applicant claims to be is the most important aspect of the recruiting process. You can verify academic and professional credentials yourself, with costs up to $100 per verification, but by interviewing candidates whose credentials have already been verified, you will save countless hours in conducting your own background checks. Credential verification is consolidated into two or three service companies that can be found on the Internet. If your institution has a contract for this service, no additional cost may be involved. Otherwise, the cost could be several hundred dollars. eInstructors.Inc, however, provides credential verification as part of its "value-added" referral service.

Some online programs recruit faculty by using an application form posted on their public Web sites. Other programs recruit faculty by using referrals from lead faculty (this is the best) and adjunct faculty (this is the next best). However you plan to recruit your instructors, require a thorough application and interview process to ensure faculty compatibility. A submitted application places applicants on the record, and the interview, usually conducted by phone, will give you an indication of whether the applicant will fit well into the academic community you are building.

Your goal is to recruit once and retain always, but occasionally you will hire someone who does not work out. This is one reason for hiring instructors as independent contractors, with a one-time contract for a set period. You are not obligated to keep an instructor beyond the contract's expiration. The

contracts, however, normally do not have provisions for termination before their expiration.

Online programs with effective procedures for recruiting instructors encounter very few instances where the performance of a first-time instructor does not warrant a future contract. But no screening process is perfect. Possible reasons why you would not invite an instructor to teach again are poor communication skills with students, failure to grade and provide feedback in a timely manner, and excessive absences during the instructor training period.

New Instructors and Your E-Learning Software

New instructors without online experience come to you with no preconceived notions of how to teach online. They are open to direction, and they welcome assistance in adapting course content to the online formats best suited for the subject matter and course materials. New instructors will not want to tinker with your e-learning software or attempt to post materials themselves. They may already suspect that the software has subtle nuances of which only the developers and trained specialists are aware.

But because you want to be certain of preserving the current content and formats of your online courses—especially, as time goes on, your well-refined cloned courses—the software's "no edit" attribute should always be activated. Only FACEs should have the ability to change content and formats inside the courses. If corrections or edits are needed for a course, they are forwarded to the FACE assigned to the course. Annually, however, major changes can be made by the course teaching team and the FACE together.

Lead faculty instructors can on their own authorize changes in their course content once a year. They first obtain

input from the affected adjunct instructors, those teaching other sections of the course. The content matrix is updated if courses materially change. In order to maintain course quality and integrity, lead faculty instructors may at any time work with the FACE to change content that is wrong, confusing, or out-of-date.

Determining Academic Rank for Instructors

Your institution should grant the same academic rank to your instructors that they hold at their home institutions, with the exception, of course, that any instructors tenured at their home institutions would not be tenured at your institution.

In constructing your online courses, all faculty persons inside all courses are given the designation "instructor." But in the faculty section of your Web site, where all instructors are listed, include each instructor's actual rank. For an instructor who is a *practitioner* and does not hold academic rank at any institution, the program director recommends a rank consistent with the instructor's achievements. The dean acts on the PD's recommendation, either approving it or assigning other rank.

Provide every instructor with a printed certificate that attests to the instructor's academic rank at your institution. Have the certificate signed and dated by your institution's president, the dean, and the program director. Then have the certificate framed and sent to the instructor following completion of the instructor's very first course.

What Do Instructors Do?

Initially, you will recruit instructors to teach a specific course—one section, from 20 to 30 students—once a year. The one-section limit should stay in effect for the first three or four years of your school's operation, or until your registrations reach

several hundred students. In this way you can have a relatively larger number of instructors early in your operations. A larger initial faculty has several advantages, one of them being an immediate infusion of vitality into your program, giving it a presence and drawing the interest of others. Having many instructors rather than only a few also makes it less likely any of them will try to influence the others in joining an effort to make contract-related demands, which would place both you and your institution in an awkward position.

But as registrations in your online programs increase, your instructors will take on an expanded role. And registrations could rise quickly. Many new online programs have seen their registrations for a given term double each year. The number of students registering for the fall term of one year, for example, could well be twice the number who registered for the fall term of the previous year.

With growing registrations, your instructors will see increased teaching duties. Many instructors will start teaching more than one section a year. But, at this point, do not allow your lead faculty instructors to teach more than two sections a year. You will need them for other duties as you continue to grow. Adjunct instructors, however, may teach several sections a year. Use the following guideline: Allow adjunct instructors to teach two or three sections the same term, but allow them no more than two contracts in any one year. Again, you want to limit individual faculty control over your program. You want to be able to manage your online programs from the top down.

The Value of Instructor Training

When recruiting prospective instructors, have them complete an "Online Skills Assessment," a simple questionnaire

about their software knowledge and computer experience. Most computers come with Microsoft products installed, so consider using Microsoft applications as your principal software. Query the prospective instructors about Microsoft Word, Excel, and PowerPoint, and ask them about their experience in using e-mail, file transfer protocol (FTP), and audio files. You can use the same questionnaire to obtain each instructor's e-mail address and the type of Internet connection used, e.g., dial-up, DSL, cable, T1, satellite. The faster the Internet connection, the faster files can be transmitted. Encourage your instructors to use their home institutional e-mail address, which usually conforms to the "name@university.edu" format. This will be the address posted inside the instructor's course on your Web site. Your administration will use this same address for sending personnel communications and other official information. Because the "name@university.edu" format identifies each instructor's home institution, your new program will gain added respectability through association.

Having a training program in place will help in recruiting and retaining instructors. Develop an *initial training and orientation session* for familiarizing your new instructors to the online environment. Before the beginning of each semester or term, schedule the training and orientation session by live webcast. Have all first-time instructors attend, and also invite your other instructors to participate, as many as the session can hold. A FACE coordinates the webcast, contacting the participating instructors by phone to help them with computer set-up and the configuration of firewalls, pop-up blockers, spam blockers, and anti-spyware software. During the webcast, the FACE explains the features of your e-learning software. The session should run about one hour, but it can be extended if the instructors desire.

Most commercial e-learning software (e.g., eCollege, WebCT, Blackboard, Oracle) provides online tutorials for instructors, giving them a view of online formats and guidance on course navigation. Since the FACE does all the behind-the-scenes work with the software, your instructors do not need to know its intricacies. Instead, the instructors learn only about the software's presentation capabilities, how courses will be viewed by students. For instructors who want to learn about technical aspects of the software, you could have your FACE offer them training at a later time.

Because most of your first-time instructors will have had no online teaching experience, some may have apprehensions about whether they can teach successfully online. Your initial training and orientation session, as well as subsequent ones, will give them the confidence that they can.

Subsequent instructor training is offered during online "faculty meetings." Schedule faculty meetings quarterly by live webcasts, using the first five to 15 minutes of each meeting to present refresher material and one new technique. Ongoing faculty training contributes to the improvement of your online programs, and accreditors require it. Documenting the training is an easy task, since the faculty meeting webcasts can be archived. Be sure to select an e-learning application that can archive all components of your webcasts, including chat, PowerPoint presentations, and audio files. You will not need to transcribe faculty meetings to meet the documentation requirements of your regional accrediting agency. Regional accreditors may sometimes ask for transcripts, but their published policies and procedures do not require them. Becoming knowledgeable of your regional agency's accreditation handbook and supplementary manuals will serve you in many ways.

You could also offer an *on-campus instructor training seminar*, preferably in conjunction with graduation or another significant event. You should invite your instructors to graduation even if you do not schedule a training seminar. As part of building a faculty community, offer to pay the lodging, meal, and travel expenses for all instructors who wish to attend. If you do schedule a training seminar, have it take place two or three days before, rather than after, the commencement ceremonies. Scheduling in this order gives your instructors a highpoint on which to end their visit. Staying an extra day or two after graduation to attend a training session will not be appealing to them. Because the instructors are independent contractors, they are not compensated for attending an on-campus training seminar. Cover only their expenses. Request that instructors confirm attendance six months in advance, and then make the hotel, seminar hall, and other arrangements.

Developing Model Faculty Contracts

The contract is a communication with your instructors, and in every communication with instructors you want to show they are valued. The quality of your communications with them over time will influence instructor retention. The wording of faculty contracts, then, should reflect the respect you hold for your instructors. Prepare a well-written and carefully structured contract that formally states the terms of agreement.

At first, you will need a model contract for only your lead faculty instructors. Later, as you engage adjunct instructors to teach the courses developed by the lead faculty, you will need another, slightly different model contract. The model contract for adjunct faculty will be basically the same as the model contract for lead faculty, but without the language related to the development of the course.

Begin with the standard "whereas" section. Here you set forth the general parameters of the agreement. This section will:

1. Name the parties making the agreement. The parties are your institution and the instructor.

2. State the independent contractor status of the instructor: "*Name of instructor*, an independent contractor according to the Internal Revenue Service (IRS) and the federal Fair Labor Standards Act (FLSA) guidelines, voluntarily wishes to teach for *corporate name of your institution* by entering into this work-made-for-hire agreement."

3. State the desire of the institution to use the instructor's services: "*Corporate name of your institution* desires to engage the teaching services of a qualified instructor for offering a course of study to students." Here, "qualified" means that the instructor has the knowledge and skills to teach the course, and that the instructor's credentials have been verified.

4. For a lead faculty person, state also the instructor's desire and ability to develop a course as directed by the administration. Also state the institution will retain ownership of the course, and that the institution may offer the course taught by other instructors to distance education students whenever and wherever the institution desires. Be clear that the contract is for both developing the course, for which you should allow about nine months, and for teaching it during the term immediately following completion of the development work.

5. Acknowledge that the contract places no restrictions on the instructor with regard to employment or contracts with other entities.

6. State that any of the instructor's existing intellectual property used in the course remains the property of the

instructor, and that any new intellectual property the instructor may create for the course will also belong to the instructor, who may use it in any other endeavor where scholarly work is required.

The next section lists the various other terms of the contract, including:

1. *Definitions.* Define the words and phrases that have a particular meaning as used in the contract. A clear set of definitions serves to eliminate misunderstandings.

2. *Scope of Work.* Describe the position-related requirements and responsibilities the instructor must meet. This is the heart of the contract, the part that states your institution's expectations of the instructor. Your list of requirements and responsibilities should include:

a. A knowledge of the e-learning software you use.

b. For lead faculty, the development of course content consistent with the goals, objectives, and description of the course, including the goals and objectives for each unit of the course. The process by which instructors may carry out the development of course content is an expression of their intellectual freedom. The contract states your institution's expectations of the instructor, not the manner in which the instructor fulfills the expectations.

c. The preparation of all the components of the course, including but not limited to the syllabus, reading and work assignments, and evaluation mechanisms such as quizzes and exams.

d. Direct interaction with students through e-mail, phone, online chat sessions, online forums, and webcasts.

e. Collaboration with the FACE in the online presentation of course materials, lectures, and slide-audio presentations.

f. Submission of course materials to the administration for

a quality-assurance approval before the start of the course, to ensure fulfillment of accreditation requirements with regard to content.

g. Completion of teaching-related tasks in a timely manner, including but not limited to the grading of tests and papers, the assignment of final grades to students, and the completion of student-record forms.

The next section of the contract outlines the support services, training, orientation, and resources that your institution will provide. Include the e-learning software, the FACE's technical support, the initial pre-term orientation and training session, the ongoing training, and any other service or resources you intend to offer.

As mentioned earlier, the proper term for the contract you will offer your instructors is a "work-made-for-hire contract." In the case of lead faculty, the institution engages the instructor as an independent contractor for a specific project— to develop and teach a particular course. A contract of this kind automatically grants ownership of the final product, the course, to the institution. The contract, however, should also state this fact. Instructors will then clearly understand that the rights to the course will belong only to the institution. A work-made-for-hire contract allows the institution to offer the course to future students, taught by other instructors, without having to pay a royalty to the lead faculty instructor who developed the course.

The contract includes an *Instructor's Warranty* section. In this section, the instructor affirms that the intellectual property used in the development of the course is entirely the work of the instructor, who has the sole right to use that intellectual property.

The *Financial Obligations* section states the amount you will

pay for the instructor's services, as well as how and when you will make payment. Normally, both lead and adjunct faculty instructors are paid at the completion of their contracts, after all grades and student-record forms are in the possession of the institution.

Earlier, the author suggested compensation of $3,000 per course for lead faculty instructors and compensation of one-half that amount, or $1,500 per course, for adjunct faculty instructors. You could also include in lead faculty contracts several circumstances that would warrant additional remuneration. For sections that normally consist of 20 students, as one example, pay a lead faculty instructor $100 for each student over 20, up to a total of 40. You could also pay the instructor to teach additional sections of the course, at $1,500 per section. As your online programs grow and you have many adjunct faculty instructors under the oversight of your original lead faculty, consider paying your lead faculty instructors $500 for each adjunct instructor under them. Finally, pay lead faculty instructors additional remuneration for assisting with capstone evaluations and for any role they take in preparing accreditation documents.

Be generous to your faculty. Treat them with respect and honor their contributions to your institution. Even if your instructor compensation is high in comparison to other online programs, the total your institution will spend for online instructors would still be much less than the costs of employing an equivalent base of full-time faculty members for on-campus instruction.

4.
Students

Applying Marketing Principles to Recruiting Online Students

S tudents who enroll in online programs generally differ from students in campus-based programs in two significant ways: The online students as a group are older and, unlike most students in campus-based programs, they have extensive family and work commitments. Your student recruiting efforts, then, are also going to differ from your institution's usual approach to recruiting students.

Begin planning your recruiting efforts a year before the enrollment of your first students. You will not use the customary techniques that colleges and universities employ for recruiting on-campus students. College fairs and career days are effective in recruiting students still in high school, but most prospective online students are well beyond high school. At the author's school, the average age of the online students, with about 53 percent of them women, was 36.

You also will not be citing in your recruiting literature the aspects of your institution that would be attractive to prospective on-campus students but of no interest to future online students. Impressive library holdings, a picturesque campus, a well-equipped recreation center, a strong intercollegiate athletic program, and excellent food service

will not matter to prospective online students. But it is very true that the overall reputation of your institution will attract them. A successful student-recruiting effort will emphasize the educational quality for which your institution is known.

By developing your online programs with students in mind, your programs will also have other built-in appeal. They will be programs that students want, taught by instructors well qualified by their credentials and experience. The courses will be offered in ways that allow for a high level of student-instructor interaction, while accommodating students' differing schedules.

In business, marketing managers know a high-quality product is not enough to ensure a company's success. A good product is essential, but success also depends on either taking the product to the customer or bringing the customer to the product. In this case, you will discover your customers—your prospective students—are already looking for your product. You need only place the information about your product—your program offerings—where you can be sure the prospective students will find it.

Most people looking for information about online educational programs use Internet search engines, such as Google and Yahoo. The presence of your school on the Internet, with your Web site submitted to the popular search engines, gives prospective students immediate access to the information you wish them to have.

The highly refined methodology of developing marketing leads online, known as "digital lead generation," is also an effective way to find prospective students for your online programs. Digital lead generation, or DLG, was first used to recruit students by the University of Phoenix Online, one of the larger online universities. DLG has since become an industry

of its own, led by companies like QuinStreet and Monster. Directory services like ClassesUSA, WorldWideLearn, and eLearners are refining and focusing their methods so clients may be able to "dial" the number of prospective students they wish to reach each month. If you plan to contract for these services, be prepared to manage communications with large numbers of prospective students. Your institution will need systems in place to answer questions about financial aid and to process applications for admission. Do not implement DLG without first attending to the infrastructure necessary to support it.

You may want to use several DLG services to meet your enrollment needs. These services can be expensive, however, ranging from $18 to several hundred dollars per qualified lead. A qualified lead is a person who meets your qualifiers as determined by the person's online answers to certain questions. The accuracy of the person's answers to your questions is not verified. You pay for all leads who meet your qualifiers whether or not the person actually enrolls.

An Interactive Online Application Form

An important element of the student-recruiting infrastructure is the *application form*. Design a form that is easy to complete, and make it readily accessible online. The Adobe Acrobat "fill-in-the-form" format allows prospective students to enter the requested information for online submission. Your form should have built-in checks for the appropriate information and required fields. A date field should be restricted to a date format, a yes-or-no question should not allow any other or both answers, and alerts should appear whenever a required field is left blank or the information is incomplete.

Submitted application forms are distributed to the appropriate administrative support offices at your institution.

These include the admissions office, the registrar's office, and the financial-aid office. Or, if your institution uses a centralized student information system (SIS) for interoffice sharing of student records, the applications would become part of the SIS database. An SIS is designed specifically for storing and retrieving student records, not for accounting purposes or invoicing for tuition and fees. Two of the many developers of SIS software are PeopleSoft and Jenzibar.

Your institution's admissions office will need to be prepared for a great increase in applications. The financial-aid office will also experience a surge in applications for loans, as a high percentage of online students apply for financial assistance. Too often, institutions are reluctant to provide the additional personnel needed to fully support larger enrollments. Because you will want applications for enrollment in your programs processed quickly and accurately, maintain close communications with your admissions office, financial-aid office, and all other affected administrative offices. Keep them updated on what to expect in terms of increased workloads.

Your Student Counselor: A Marketing Professional

Hire a full-time *student counselor*, or student recruiter, to follow up on the leads from the DLG services. Place an ad with Monster or one of the other major online job-placement services. Large online institutions hire and train hundreds of student counselors every year, and many move from institution to institution. Try to hire an experienced recruiter, one who already has several thousand dollars worth of training. You may need to replace your recruiter several times before you find someone who fits well into your school, but a careful screening process will improve the chances of hiring the right person the first time.

The foremost attribute of an effective student counselor is honesty. You will not want someone who gives prospective students inaccurate information or makes promises you cannot fulfill.

The student counselor you hire must have the ability to relate exceptionally well over the phone with strangers. Most of the student counselor's work will entail calling the prospective students identified by your DLG services. A good student counselor, then, possesses the qualities of a good sales person, and someone whose enthusiasm is not dampened by rejection. For every 100 DLG prospects, only three or four will eventually enroll, and it usually takes several calls from the student counselor to move these few into the application process.

Your student counselor will also need computer skills to record the tracking data necessary for follow-up and hand-off to others. ACT software, a contact management application, can be adapted for storing the tracking data on prospective students. The student counselor will collect a large amount of data about each prospective student, from the time of the first inquiry to the submission of an application. Another attribute of an effective student counselor, then, is an ability to keep detailed and accurate records.

During the first few months of using online digital lead recruitment, you will need to adjust your systems often, discarding the mechanisms that prove unproductive and experimenting with new ones. Keep registration projections at an attainable level. As stated earlier, a doubling of registrations each comparable term during the first few years of a new online program is not an unreasonable expectation.

Shaping Your Image on the Web

Another important source of prospective students will be your public *Web site.* Your presence on the Internet will place you directly in front of anyone looking for information about online programs in any of the disciplines you will be offering. Because most prospective students will at first measure the quality of your programs by your Web site, its appearance and content, as mentioned before, must make a highly positive impression on everyone who visits it.

Using *content management software* to create and maintain your public Web site is more efficient and costs less than using traditional HTML coding and individual page creation. As your site grows, you will need to store information for presentation in various formats. Content management software, like Macromedia's Contribute3, enables you to store information as a master document and then use the information wherever it may be needed on your Web site. For example, your "Contact Us" page holds numerous names with e-mail addresses, which change often. By using a content management software application, you can edit an e-mail address once and have the change appear in all places where it is used on your site.

The Web site for your online programs should serve as a portal for your institution's library, financial-aid office, and admissions office. Also include links to your institution's policies, procedures, and student handbook, as well as a page for "Frequently Asked Questions." Giving future and current students access to detailed information helps prevent misunderstandings.

Construct your site with a home page that presents general information common to all your online programs. Give visitors the option of entering one of two clearly distinct

primary sections of the site, one for current students and one for prospective students. Then divide each section into appropriate subsections. Within the section for prospective students, you will need subsections with information on tuition and fees, admission requirements, applying for admission, and obtaining financial aid. Within the section for current students, you will need subsections for each course, the calendar, and process information. Place a login route on your home page for your current students. They can enter their user names and passwords to access their courses and other information intended only for current students.

Structure your site for ease of use. Visitors should be able to find the information they are looking for with no more than three mouse clicks.

Give your home page special attention. Prospective students visiting it the first time will form an immediate impression of your institution's online offerings based on the page's graphics, writing style, and content. Allow visitors to access the various sections of your site with one click. Besides the two primary sections for prospective and current students, allow public access to sections for news, faculty profiles, student information resources, and accreditation. Routinely review the home page and the public sections once a month, updating them as needed.

Placing a demonstration course on your Web site is an effective way to engage the interest of prospective students. A well-produced demo will give them an understanding of the e-learning process and show them its effectiveness. It will also diminish the resistance people normally have about trying something new. Many e-learning software vendors provide a demo course at costs ranging from $1,000 to $2,000. The

demo course should be accessible by all visitors to your home page, without the need to enter a user name and password.

Your Web site will be your advertisement to the world. It can be a powerful draw upon prospective students by projecting the high quality of your programs. Give every detail of your site careful attention. Show an awareness of your main audience—older students who have full-time jobs and families. Make certain the text is letter perfect. Subject your site to several pre-launch reviews by others. Do not place it on the Web until you are confident it represents the very best your institution can produce.

Attracting International Students

In preparing the application instructions for your public Web site, keep in mind prospective *international applicants.* You can make your online programs inviting to prospective applicants outside the U.S. by mentioning that your institution offers a foreign transcript evaluation service and, as your programs mature, you could cite the percentage of international students enrolled in your programs to indicate that you welcome students from other countries.

English is the world-wide language of education, and it is not necessary to translate your course materials into other languages for foreign students. Because your admissions requirements will include the Test of English as a Foreign Language (TOEFL), all your international students will be able to read, speak, and write English.

Bolstering Student Retention Through Service

Efforts that support student retention are as important as those that support student recruiting. The high drop-out rates that many online programs experience can be avoided

by relying on strategies designed to retain the students you worked so hard to recruit.

One way to help ensure high retention is to foster student satisfaction by offering the services that online students need as they complete their courses and move toward their certificates and degrees. For example, should the availability of texts by the start date become an issue, pre-approve through the publisher and have ready to fax the first two or three chapters so students do not have a delay in their studies. Be ready to help your students in any way you can. This is not to say you should make your programs easy for students to complete. To the contrary, your programs must be challenging or students will feel they are not receiving their money's worth.

Most drops occur during the first ten days of a course. Consultants who work in the field of online education generally agree the national drop-out average for online courses is about 25 percent. Students drop courses for many different reasons, but probably one of the more common is a fear of being unable to complete the course successfully. To help counter student uncertainties and apprehensions, assign a student adviser to every new student as soon as the student is approved for admission. The student adviser from that point on replaces the student recruiting counselor as the student's primary contact person at your institution. Your student advisers should take a proactive approach, calling the students rather than waiting for the students to call them. The advisers encourage the students to call or e-mail them whenever questions or concerns arise. A student adviser who cannot answer a question finds someone who can. They are trained professionals, often in the field of public relations, and they are highly knowledgeable of your programs and the resources available to students. More about the role of student advisors appears later in this chapter.

Once students have completed three or four courses toward their certificates or degrees, they are much less likely to drop out of future courses. They have become vested. The primary focus of your retention efforts will logically be on your newer students, but always give every student the best possible service. Your reputation for providing services will result in referrals of new students from current and former students. Superior services benefit both retention and recruiting.

Students who leave your institution before program completion are said to have "exited" your institution. With effective retention strategies, the percentage of exits among students in your online programs can be as low as one percent. But you will not be able to keep everyone. Some individuals lack the personal qualities necessary to succeed in an online program. But the percentage of your students who exit will be small if you accept only those who show evidence of initiative, drive, and self-discipline.

High completion rates will speak well of your programs, further contributing to your ability to recruit good students. Your regional accrediting agency will also be pleased, because high completion rates demonstrate student satisfaction. Low completion rates, however, would tell an accreditor that students may not only be dissatisfied, but perhaps your programs are accepting too many unqualified students. Accreditors dislike high exit rates because they indicate many students are spending money on tuition without ever earning a credential, money which the students likely borrowed under a federal loan program for which they were eligible because your institution is accredited. Because of the significant impacts that retention has on finances and accreditation, strategies to retain students must be a part of your planning process from the beginning.

Giving students an *academic plan* will enable them to

visualize their progression through the courses to the final attainment of a certificate or degree. An academic plan will provide direction for students and help them set a goal of completing your program within a certain time frame. Without an academic plan, even older students have difficulty seeing the final result of their efforts. Preparing an academic plan for each student will increase retention by giving every student a visible, attainable goal.

A student's academic plan considers the specific degree or certificate program the student has selected, the courses the student must take, and the academic terms during which those courses will be offered. The academic plan should be part of the discussions between the student recruiting counselor and the prospective student, and later between the student adviser and the enrolled student. At every juncture in the student's studies, the adviser and student review the plan together and make adjustments as desired or necessary. Make each student's academic plan accessible to the student through your Web site.

The Distinction Between Enrolled and Registered Students

Approving applicants for enrollment is an admissions function. Chapter 5, on "Administration," includes information on admission requirements, policies, procedures, and your interactions with your institution's admission office. An applicant for any of your online programs who is admitted to the institution is considered for your purposes to be "enrolled." These students submitted their applications, paid their application fees, went through the admissions review process, and were accepted for admission. Newly enrolled students often do not immediately sign up, or "register," for the courses they will take. Some may delay taking any courses

until several academic terms later. A distinction is made, then, between enrolled students and registered students. Enrolled students may change their minds about attending and not ever register.

Categories of enrolled students include:

- *Never Entered*—Applied to students who never register for any courses. Allow a fairly long period to elapse— it could be as long as seven or eight years—before removing a never-entered student from enrollment.
- *Withdrawn*—Applied to students who register and pay the tuition but then cancel their registrations, or withdraw, before the start of their courses. These students remain enrolled because they are eligible to register again for future terms without submitting another application for admission.
- *Dropped*—Applied to students who register and pay the tuition but later, after the start date for courses, drop their courses. These students also remain enrolled, as they may register for future terms.
- *Registered*—Applied to students who have signed up for courses, paid the tuition, and are taking courses. Students register for courses online, signing up at any time for a course to be offered during the upcoming term. Encourage students to follow their academic plans. Have a policy in place that requests students to inform their advisers if they will not be registering for the upcoming term because of family, work, or other obligations. Online students often need to depart from their academic plans and skip a term or two. Have a mechanism in place for staying aware of each student's intentions.

Two other categories apply to formerly enrolled students:

- *Exited*—Applied to students who formally request separation from your institution. These students are removed from enrollment.
- *Disappeared*—Applied to students who stop participating in their course work before completing the program, without giving notice or any reasons, and who do not respond to efforts to contact them.

Chapter 5 has additional information on enrollment and registration.

Student Advisers: Your Service Department

The best avenues of service your programs can have are its student advisers. For newer students particularly, an adviser can make their introduction to the world of online learning a pleasant and rewarding experience.

The student adviser is each student's single point of contact at your institution. The adviser helps new students adjust to the online learning experience, easing any apprehensions the students may have. This full-time staff person should be a congenial, helpful person who can become a "friend" and advocate for students. Up to 400 students may be assigned to an adviser. As enrollment increases, hire additional advisers as needed. When your first adviser has 400 students, assign 200 of them to a newly hired second adviser. You will then have two advisers to whom you can assign a total of 400 more students. When each has 400 students again, take 100 students from each and assign them to a newly hired third adviser.

Communications between advisers and their students are mostly by phone. Provide advisers with a brief profile of each new student assigned to them, including phone numbers and best times to call. Student advisers will work mostly during evening hours and on weekends, since most students will be at

work during weekdays. Advisers should be salaried employees, thereby avoiding the costs of overtime.

The orientation session for new students, an important student service, was covered in Chapter 2. Again, your goal for the session is to acclimate new students to your online learning environment and, more importantly, to instill in them confidence and enthusiasm for achieving the goals they have set for themselves. In this way you are, perhaps without the students realizing it, being of service to them. At the same time, you are helping to ensure high retention rates for your programs. Make the session mandatory for all new students, and open the live webcast to any current students who would like to attend. Take attendance at the session so follow-up can occur for those unable to participate.

Risk Assessment: Helping Students Succeed

Develop written procedures for risk assessment and apply them to all students who enroll. For each student, track the factors associated with dropping out. Knowing which students are at risk of dropping out will enable you to work with their student advisers in applying intervention measures.

Begin planning for systematic risk assessment early. Your procedures should include the monitoring of each student for signs of possible failure and recording the information. Develop a system that signals an alert for the student adviser whenever a student becomes a high risk.

Factors commonly associated with failure or dropping out are:

- *A low GPA for previous work.* New students whose GPAs at the bachelor's level were significantly lower than the average for enrolled students have a greater risk of failing or dropping out.

- *Not attending your orientation session.* New students who skip the session and do not reschedule before the start of their courses are more likely to withdraw from or drop their courses.
- *Not viewing the demonstration course.* Most e-learning software can monitor whether prospective students view the demo course on your Web site. Experience has shown that new students who have not viewed the demo are more likely to drop out.
- *Late registration.* Registering after the deadline is a major indicator of risk.
- *Slowness in obtaining textbooks.* Students who procrastinate in obtaining their textbooks may not be fully committed to your online program. Those who do not have their textbooks by the course start date are at a risk.
- *Lateness in completing financial-aid forms.* Not submitting the forms by the deadline is a significant sign of risk. Committed students consider their financial aid a high priority. Generally, only students not fully committed would delay completing the forms.

Your monitoring system may include a scale for assessing each student's risk, from "very high" to "very low." Students with a "very high" assessment should be intervened first. Direct communication with the student is required, which may be initiated by the student adviser, the course instructor or, when appropriate, the FACE. Often students simply need reassurance, but sometimes they are experiencing serious difficulties. The earlier a student receives help in addressing any problems, the greater the chances for success.

Providing Students with Financial-Aid Information

Students enrolled in online degree programs within

regionally accredited institutions may apply for federally insured student loans. Eligible students include those who are either at least half time or those who are continuous time. A continuous-time student might register for only one course a term but takes courses throughout the year, without skipping any terms.

Because more than half of all online students at most accredited institutions receive financial aid, post the Free Application for Federal Student Aid (FAFSA) on your Web site for online completion and submission. Provide registered students a secure e-mail account using your institution's Web address so the award letters can be sent electronically and securely when aid is approved. Encourage students to complete the form early, allowing enough time for them to respond to follow-up communications and to receive their funds prior to the due date for tuition and fees, usually the day courses begin.

Federal financial-aid programs will not cover expenses for room and board, transportation, and other expenses normally incurred only by students in campus-based programs. Advise your online students not to expect coverage for these costs.

Setting Tuition and Fees with Students in Mind

Prospective online students tend to "price shop" for the best values. Most will look for a high-quality program where tuition and fees are less than other programs of comparable quality. Reviewing the tuition and fee structures for online programs at other institutions will help you determine the amounts you might charge, but your paramount considerations will be your revenue goals and creating market appeal. With the anticipation of doubling your registrations annually, you can calculate whether the projected revenues under a proposed

tuition and fee structure over a five-year period will be enough to cover, at a minimum, the start-up and operational costs incurred during that time. Setting tuition and fees in the middle of market, neither too high nor too low, would appeal to prospective students while producing the revenue needed to meet your goals.

Students like the convenience of being able to pay their tuition and fees over the Internet. Have your controller make the necessary arrangements for using PayPal and then promote its availability on your Web site. Also provide for credit-card payments and, for students in other countries, wire transfers.

Meeting the Technical Needs of Students

Provide guidance to students on the computer hardware and software they will need. Many of the software requirements—such as Flash, Acrobat Reader, and Shockwave—are free downloads from the Internet. Before the orientation session, encourage students to take the browser test provided by most e-learning software vendors as a way to assure the proper configuration of their computers and software.

Your FACEs serve students as their contacts for technical assistance. Ongoing technical support is vital to student success, as online students often encounter difficulties related to computer configurations. Many students need guidance in configuring firewalls, anti-virus programs, spam and pop-up blockers, and anti-spyware in order to access their courses or enter a live webcast. Besides helping students who experience access and downloading difficulties, your FACEs help students to stay current in their courses by reminding them of deadlines, due dates, and upcoming exams.

Helping Students Obtain Their Textbooks

Develop a plan for guaranteeing that students obtain their

textbooks well before the start of courses. Because impediments to a smooth distribution process are many, you will need a carefully thought-out system. You do not want a courses to begin with students and instructors frustrated because of an unavailability of texts.

Textbook distribution may take several forms. You can, for instance, include textbooks in the tuition payment and send registered students their texts directly. This is probably the best way to ensure that students receive their texts in time, but it is also costly and requires administrative oversight, a storage area, ongoing attention to inventory, and personnel for packaging and shipping.

Another way, one the author recommends, is to have students obtain their textbooks themselves. Several Web-based bookstores specialize in serving online students and will ship to the student's door within three days. If you have international students who will need a particular textbook, make sure the supplier can have the books delivered to the students' countries. Using a bookstore that drop-ships to students, such as Matthews, relieves you of a time-consuming, cumbersome, and costly task. Be sure to advise students of the bookstore they should use.

Publishers usually make desk copies of textbooks available for faculty persons, but allow ample time for delivery. Suppliers now require many more forms and verifications than in the past before they will send the free desk copies. Take the time to complete the forms, as the desk copies will help instructors decide on the text best suited for the course.

Because instructors often give their students textbook reading assignments before courses formally begin, to ensure that the first chat session is productive, you will need to require that students purchase their texts well in advance of the course

start date. Inform students at least 60 days prior to the next term of the texts they will need and where to purchase them. E-mail this information to the students as they register for their courses, and also post it on your Web site.

A word about textbook publishers: A massive consolidation is taking place within the industry, with many publishers buying other publishers. A publisher that has been providing some of your textbooks may suddenly merge with another. Keeping up with ISBN numbers and publishers can be difficult. You will need to confirm beforehand that the textbooks your students will need are available from the publisher or online bookstore you recommend, and that sufficient quantities are in stock for the anticipated demand. Publishers can also change editions at the most inopportune times, such as immediately before a term begins. Be vigilant for changes in publishers, new ISBN numbers, and discontinued stock. Be aware, too, that publishers generally require distributors to return unsold books prior to the release of a revised edition to strengthen sales of the new books. This policy can also assure the unavailability of the book you planned to use.

The Student Handbook: It Serves Administrators, Too

A detailed but concisely written student handbook developed specifically for online students is indispensable for efficient operations. The handbook, with its standards, policies, and procedures, serves both students and administrators. Online students in some regards are much like their younger on-campus counterparts: They will look for loopholes to obtain the outcomes they want. The handbook must therefore be precisely written, leaving no room for interpreting statements in any way other than their intended meaning. Yet, the

handbook should not have a dogmatic or authoritarian tone, which students would find offensive.

Topics the handbook covers include but are not limited to:

- *Tuition Refund Policy*—Include a table that shows the differing percentages of tuition that will be refunded to students who withdraw from a course before it starts or drop a course during the first, second, and third weeks of the term. State any other circumstances that would entitle students to full or partial refunds. Usually, only refunds of tuition are made. Fees normally are not refundable.

- *Communications*—E-mail is an appropriate and the most efficient way to exchange written communications with online students. Assign every registered student an institutional e-mail account that uses your Web address. The institution maintains the student accounts to ensure they are secure, virus free, and protected from hackers. Include in your communications policy a requirement that students use their institutional accounts for written communications with personnel at your institution, and that the institution's written communications to them will be sent to these same accounts.

- *Grading*—Establish a grading scale, typically A, B, C, D, and F, and publish it in the handbook. Define each grade with a corresponding percentage scale where, for example, a student with an overall course average of between 90 and 100 percent would receive an A for the course. You should also include descriptions of the evaluation tools your programs employ in assessing student learning, noting that instructors

provide information in their course materials about the specific methods they use. Evaluation tools are discussed in Chapter 2.

- *Capstone Requirements*—A capstone that both satisfies accreditors and has the flexibility for meeting the needs of online students was described in Chapter 2. Publish a detailed description of your capstone in the student handbook, making clear the attributes it must have.

- *Graduation*—List the requirements for graduation: completion of the required courses with an overall GPA of B or better, and within a time frame consistent with accreditation or state requirements, typically seven years; payment of all financial obligations; and satisfactory completion of the capstone. Include information about your school's graduation ceremonies, discussed in Chapter 5.

- *Academic Probation*—Use precise terms in defining academic probation. Explicitly set forth the circumstances that will place a student on probation, and the conditions that will remove it.

- *Academic Dismissal*—State without any ambiguity the circumstances that will result in a student's dismissal for poor academic performance.

- *Academic Appeal Procedure*—Specify in the handbook the various methods for appealing a grade and the forms or letters required, and state the final authority. Higher learning institutions usually have a three-level appeal process. The first is a student appeal to the instructor; the second is a written appeal to the program director who reviews and renders a decision; the third a written appeal to the dean, whose decision is final.

- *Performance Standards*—Use the handbook for presenting to students the characteristics you expect them to possess with regard to intellectual, conceptual, behavioral, social, and communications skills and abilities. Include a requirement that students self-assess their compliance and affirm that they satisfy your standards. Information on developing performance standards appears in Chapter 5.
- *Code of Conduct*—Include statements on cheating, plagiarism, failing to report violations by others, and the misrepresentation of information on applications, in courses, and at examinations. Add any other statements you believe may be appropriate for your online students and not covered in other policies.
- *Harassment Policy*—A published harassment policy has unfortunately become mandatory in today's world. The policy should state in general terms the parameters of harassment and then list specific examples, such as stalking, unwelcome communications, comments or actions of a sexual nature, and aspersions related to gender, race, ethnicity, or religion.
- *Disciplinary Sanctions*—List the sanctions your disciplinary committee may impose for violations of policies and the Code of Conduct. Include denial of admission, denial of registration, a written reprimand, course failure or a grade reduction, and dismissal from the institution.
- *Glossary*—In this section of the handbook, define the key terms as you have used them. Give them precise definitions so the meaning of terms as they appear in the handbook will be open to only one interpretation.

The student handbook may be posted on your Web site, with a notice to new students upon their acceptance that it is available for review and downloading. Mention in your notice the topics covered in the handbook and emphasize the importance of the information it contains.

Students as Customers

Your enrollments and the overall completion rate for your online degree and certificate programs will reflect the quality of the services and support your students receive, from the time of your first contact with them until they submit their capstone. Among many educational administrators, students are considered the counterpart of customers in the business world. The formula for the success of your online programs is analogous: Develop a superior product, market it well to your target audience, and provide excellent service.

5.

Administration

Obtaining the Support of Your Institution's Leadership

Administrative support for a proposed online school begins at the top. In other words, first obtain the support of your institution's president and governing board members. Even better, obtain their *enthusiastic* support, so much so that they actually issue a directive for starting the school rather than merely approve a proposal that you submit.

Why is it so important to have support from your institution's leadership? The answer lies in the unfortunate reality that detractors of online education can be found among the faculty and administration of most traditional institutions of higher learning. Some campus-based educators still consider online educational programs inferior to the classroom educations they received. They cite different reasons in support of their perceptions, but generally they are unaware of the innovations taking place in online education.

Other traditional educators have been prejudiced by the so-called online universities and colleges that offer degrees even at the doctoral level with very little or no study required. The one real requirement for their degrees is a credit card. Of course, these are not institutions of any distinction, and they lack true accreditation. They usually claim accreditation, but their accreditors are not recognized by the Secretary of Education or

the Council for Higher Education Accreditation. These online schools are in effect selling degrees. They are not really online schools at all, but online shams. Some administrators and faculty members shy away from proposals for online programs at their institutions because of a concern that the public may associate the programs with the bogus online schools.

Before you begin promoting your online plans, arm yourself with studies that validate the effectiveness of online education. Provide trustees, top administrators, and key faculty members with research findings that vouch for the high level of academic performance by online students and the success graduates have in the job market. The doubters will ask about cheating and other problems they perceive as unique to online programs. Gather the research and promote its findings: that online education, if done properly, can be as effective as campus-based education, with the advantage that it reaches out to and can benefit great numbers of prospective students who otherwise could not further their educations. The support of your institution's leadership will be invaluable in obtaining an adequate start-up budget and in moving your programs forward despite any opposition from unsupportive administrators or faculty members.

Some of your institution's administrators who do not oppose online education itself may resist your plans for reasons more related to basic human nature. They simply may not want to take on more obligations with no guarantee of additional resources and pay. They will realize your programs, if successful, will mean more applicants, more students, and more work.

You will also need the finesse it takes to navigate the political currents that flow through virtually every institution of any kind. A good knowledge of the politics at play within

your institution will keep you clear of any submerged rubble. You may have the support of close colleagues and, more importantly, the support of top administrators, but be very careful of those who may be wielding political clubs behind the scenes. Know your institution's politics and align yourself with those who make the decisions and can maneuver a proposal through any undercurrents critics might create.

Your Institution's Administrative Support Services

Efficiency in the administration of your online programs will require reliance on the centralized support services of your institution. In preparing your administrative blueprint, plan that the offices and departments that make up the infrastructure of your institution will serve your online school in the same ways they serve the institution's other schools and programs. The three university-wide offices upon which you will most rely, and with which you will most interact, are the admissions office, the registrar's office, and the financial-aid office.

The Role of Admissions Personnel

Your institution's *admissions office* will play an especially significant role in the success of your online programs. It will be the first of your institution's centralized support services to feel the impact of your programs. The anticipated large annual increases in applications for your online programs will demand more admissions personnel as time goes on, and your awareness of this need and a willingness on the part of the institution's leadership to create staff positions as warranted will alleviate the concerns of admissions administrators.

Admissions personnel have the responsibility of collecting and recording the information needed to determine whether an applicant qualifies for enrollment. Although they do not

make the decision to admit an applicant, they do provide their findings to the separate admissions committees at the institution's schools. The job of the admissions office is made easier if prospective students use an interactive online application form that they electronically submit to the admissions office, as well as to the financial-aid and registrar's offices, or to a student information system that all these offices can access. The application form, as described in Chapter 4, should be posted on your Web site. Also post accompanying information on "How to Apply." Give students all the information they need to complete the application form.

Time is critical in processing applications for admission to online programs—much more so than with campus-based programs—because online students have other choices on their desktops. A courteous and helpful admissions staff will increase the chances of a prospective student's enrollment. Watch for possible deficiencies in the admissions office which would discourage prospective students, such as late replies to e-mail inquiries, not giving immediate help to callers, or slowness in evaluating applications. By at once developing and then continuing to nurture a highly positive working relationship with key admissions personnel, you will be able to impress upon them the importance of the time element in online education and suggest any needed improvements without creating ill-will.

The Application Fee

Most institutions have an *application fee*, usually between $50 and $100. The fee helps offset costs associated with processing the applications. Some students will complete applications for several institutions, but this practice is probably not as common for online programs as for campus-

based programs. If possible, have the application fees credited to your budget as income.

The Requirements for Admission

State clearly on your Web site, without room for misinterpretation, the *requirements for admission.* Develop requirements with the intent that applicants who meet them should be able to complete your programs. The requirements do not need to be elaborate so long as they will tend to preclude applications from students who lack the ability to do well. Consider including these requirements:

1. *A prerequisite degree.* For graduate-level degree and certificate programs, require a bachelor's degree. Be sure the admissions office as an established procedure for evaluating credits and degrees from foreign universities. Several educational services firms specialize in determining the U.S. equivalency of foreign educational programs.

2. *A minimum grade point average (GPA).* Set a minimum GPA for previous work, typically a cumulative for all four years of undergraduate school. The author recommends that you have admissions personnel calculate the GPA from the transcript provided by the institution that granted the applicant's bachelor's degree. This transcript likely will not include any undergraduate courses or community college courses where no degree was granted. But if you wish an applicant to submit transcripts showing all credits from all institutions, clearly state this requirement. It will, however, delay the process while the admissions office waits for an applicant's transcripts from different institutions. It will also create a barrier to admissions for those applicants who will need to contact several institutions and pay several transcript fees. In the author's experience, requiring a transcript only from the institution that granted

the undergraduate degree is quite acceptable. Another point to consider is whether to require applicants to a master's program to submit transcripts from institutions where they may have earned a doctorate. If so, this requirement also must be clearly stated. At the author's school, transcripts for graduate work above the master's degree were not required, but they were accepted when applicants voluntarily submitted them.

3. *The Test of English as a Foreign Language (TOEFL).* Students who do not have a good command of both written and spoken English generally experience significant difficulties in online educational programs, placing considerable demands on both instructors and administrators. They can impinge upon your services to other students by requiring an unreasonable amount of time and attention. As your programs grow, possibly up to half your applicants will not have English as their first language. For these applicants you need to require the TOEFL. You could, however, diminish this barrier to admissions by exempting those applicants who have had a minimum of two years of studies at a U.S. institution. Typically, institutions require a minimum score of 222 for the online TOEFL and 500 on the written test. Except for the TOEFL when required, set identical admission requirements for U.S. and international students.

4. *An application fee.* Instruct applicants to pay the non-refundable application fee in U.S. dollars when submitting the online application form, using one of your online payment options. Applicants in other countries can pay in U.S. dollars by using PayPal, a wire transfer, or a bank draft from a U.S. bank. Your application form might include a list of payment options, with instructions for the applicant to check the option used. In the case of wire transfers and bank drafts from international applicants, include a statement that the applicant will be

notified and the application processed as soon as payment is received.

Rolling Admission Dates

Online education, with its scheduling resilience and non-reliance upon physical facilities, is highly accommodating of *rolling admission dates.* The more entry dates you offer new students throughout the year, the more convenient your programs will be for adults with career and family commitments.

Individuals who make the decision to pursue online education generally want to begin their course work as soon as they can. A long delay between the time of decision and the time that courses start will likely cause prospective applicants to continue their online searches for programs that better suit their schedules. In the author's experience, prospective applicants usually do not want to wait longer than ten weeks to begin their studies. This extremely short window requires that your online programs have several entry dates during the year, usually accomplished with a "continuous course schedule" of year-round terms. Students take one course each term, with the term lasting from six to eight weeks. One term rolls into the next, separated by a weekend. The start of each new term can be an entry date for new students.

Standard, Conditional, and Probationary Admission

Most institutions have three pathways to enrollment: standard admission, conditional admission, and probationary admission. The most common of these is the *standard admission* route. An applicant who satisfies all published requirements for admission to a program is granted standard admission.

The requirements for a standard admission usually include a minimum grade point average (GPA) and—for students for

whom English is not their first language and who have not spent two years at a U.S. school—a minimum score on the TOEFL. The author recommends setting the minimum GPA at 2.5 on a 4.0 scale, with the precaution that many students who barely meet this minimum will create unreasonable demands on your instructors and staff and the likelihood of failure.

Another admission requirement some online graduate schools use is the Graduate Record Examination (GRE). Many online schools, however, have omitted the GRE as a requirement because they have found it a poor predictor of performance in an online program. The examination, with its cost and time requirements, is also for many prospective students a disincentive when deciding on whether to apply for admission.

A *conditional admission* enables a college senior to enter a graduate program before receiving a bachelor's degree. This route is usually reserved for exceptionally well-qualified candidates who are academically and personally prepared to manage the challenges of starting graduate school while still working on their bachelor's degrees. Providing a conditional admission pathway for these so-called "gunners" to enter your programs will add at least a small number of students to your enrollment figures.

A *probationary admission* allows an applicant to enroll who does not meet one or more of the standard admission requirements. Most often, these applicants are unable to satisfy the institution's minimum GPA requirement. They generally have not applied themselves previously but now realize the importance of furthering their educations. As a group, they tend to be difficult to manage in an online setting, with only a small percentage showing any improvement in their academic habits.

Applicants granted probationary admission will be more troublesome than their peers, and their demands on your services will be much greater. Additionally, your better-qualified students may become disenchanted as they become aware of the poorly qualified students in their courses. Your overall retention rate also will be lower if you accept many students with probationary status, because the poorly qualified students are the ones most likely to drop out. Your programs do not need to allow for probationary admissions, and you may be doing yourself a service by excluding it as an entry pathway. The negatives are many, the positives few.

Performance Standards

Establishing *performance standards* is as important to online education as it is to campus-based education. You can familiarize yourself with various models used at other institutions by doing an online search for "Performance Standards and Higher Education."

Having performance standards will protect your institution by prescribing the skills and abilities students need to participate in your programs. Without a carefully written set of performance standards, situations could arise where a governmental agency would require your institution to furnish a student with expensive specialized computers or software, or even to provide side-by-side assistance. Involve your institution's legal services in the development of your performance standards.

Your "Student Count": The Number of Registered Students

The *registration* process for online education programs, as pointed out in the previous chapter, is not the same as the enrollment process. During the somewhat lengthy enrollment

process, a prospective student submits an application form, pays the application fee, and has transcripts as required by your admissions policy and any other required documents sent to the admissions office. The admissions office verifies the information it receives, evaluates the student's qualifications, and then forwards its findings to your school's admissions committee for a decision. Admitted students are considered enrolled students, a status they hold until they sign up—or register—for a course and pay the tuition and fees. At that point, they become registered students.

Registration, along with payment of tuition and fees, is an online process that notifies you immediately that an enrolled student will actually be taking a particular course during the upcoming term. Your "student count" is the number of students registered for any given term, less any withdrawals and drops as the term progresses. "Student count" and "enrollment" are often used synonymously, and when others ask you for your current-term enrollment figure, you will know that they mean the number of registered students. For your purposes, however, your actual online enrollment consists of all admitted students, both those currently registered and those not presently registered but who are eligible to register for future terms.

Your *student count*—the number of registered students for a term—is the number to watch as the start date for upcoming term approaches, and it is the number to chart from term to term. Tracking your student count term by term will enable you to project more accurately the number of registrations for future terms, information that will be essential to your ongoing planning process.

The Student Counselor: Your Own Recruiting Officer

The *student counselor* who functions as the recruiting officer

for your programs should report to the dean, assistant dean, or other key administrator of the online school, not to your institution's admissions director. Because of the critical role the student counselor has in the success of your programs, a direct-line reporting structure between you and the counselor facilitates effective, ongoing communications. Close supervision will strengthen the student counselor's performance and ensure that prospective students are receiving accurate information. If the student counselor were assigned to your institution's admissions office, the counselor's allegiance to your programs would not be as strong. Rather than working at your behest, the counselor would be taking directives from the institution's admissions director. Such an indirect reporting structure could lead to inefficiencies in performance, dissemination of misinformation to prospective online students, and unnecessary barriers to admission.

As discussed in the previous chapter, the student counselor will receive and follow up on the digital lead inquiries from online generator services and directories. The average daily number of inquires will depend on the service quality of your digital lead generator (DLG) contract and the attractiveness of your programs to adults interested in pursuing online educational opportunities. If the degrees and courses your school offers are highly marketable to your target audience, and the DLG services you use have a record of performing well, you may count on your student counselor having a steady flow of inquiries.

The Registrar's Office

Your institution's *registrar,* who will maintain your students' registration records and transcripts, will be a close working ally. Seek the help of your registrar's office in establishing

effective procedures to track your online students, with the goal of creating a record-keeping process free of impediments and time-consuming chores. The areas that will need attention are:

1. *Registration records.* In online education, registered students often change their minds. Online students will withdraw from courses before the start date or drop their courses afterward more frequently than their campus-based counterparts, resulting in more record keeping for the registrar's office. Develop a systemized record-keeping procedure that will facilitate numerous changes without requiring an undue amount of staff time.

2. *Transcript verification.* Your student counselor will request that prospective students send transcripts of their previous academic work to your institution's registrar. Create a procedure whereby the registrar's office can quickly and easily notify the appropriate student recruiter upon the arrival of an applicant's transcript. Work with your admissions office and registrar to formulate a policy that would grant a provisional admission to an online applicant whose transcript does not arrive in time for a standard admissions decision, with the requirement that the transcript must be received by the halfway point of the student's first term. If the transcript does not arrive by the deadline, the student is informed of an ineligibility to register for any future term until the transcript is received. By allowing prospective students to register for their first term even though their transcripts have not arrived will eliminate the possibility that you would lose these prospective students to other institutions' online programs.

3. *Recording of grades.* Early in the planning phase of your online school, establish a clear, easily understood grading scale and policy. Your grading scale could use the letter grades A

through F, and additionally you could use plus and minus letter grades. A corresponding percentage scale would determine the letter grade. Your grading policy must include the breakpoint for passing. Many graduate schools that use letter grades do not record D's, and the practice you decide upon must be included in the policy. It must also address whether a failing grade may be removed from a student's transcript if the student retakes the course and passes. Allowing for the replacement of failing grades has become a common practice but, if you adopt it, an understanding of this provision by the registrar's office, student advisers, instructors, and students is important. By establishing your grading scale and policy early in the planning process, you ensure an acceptance and understanding of them well before your first courses begin, and you help the registrar's office prepare for its recording responsibility. Your grading scale and policy, as noted in the previous chapter, are published in the student handbook.

Graduation Ceremonies

At some institutions, the coordination of graduation ceremonies is a function of the registrar's office. At other institutions, the ceremonies may be coordinated by the president's or provost's office. Sometimes each school within the larger institution has its own graduation, usually coordinated by the dean's office of each school. For an online school, a separate graduation is preferable, and you may need to seek approval from the registrar or other institutional officials to conduct your own ceremony. Having a separate graduation for your online students enables you to schedule a time and place convenient for them, and it allows for a relatively small number of attendees, which is desirable because everyone will know many others through online interactions and phone

conversations but will be meeting them in person for the first time. We had our graduation in September each year, after the fall term started.

If your institution's community is not served by a major airport, you may wish to hold your ceremony at a hotel or other facility near the closest major airport, making attendance easy for the graduating students and their guests while still enabling instructors and others from your school to attend. Having your ceremonies on campus, however, would give the graduating students a greater sense of identity with your institution. Limit family and friends to a manageable number, five to seven for each graduate. Provide a lunch for which graduating students may purchase tickets. Announce the details of the graduation ceremony about ten months before the date and obtain reservations, along with cap and gown sizes, at least six months in advance. Using paper caps and gowns is a practical alternative to using a rental service and keeps the graduation fees for students low. The graduates can take them home if they desire.

Invite all students scheduled to complete their programs before the graduation date to attend the ceremony. But do not require attendance, because for many students the expense would be excessive, creating a recruiting barrier. Prospective students who cannot easily attend a graduation ceremony would look for other programs if they were to see that you required attendance at graduation. You would also need to process records for your international students entering the U.S. on visas and track them while they are in the U.S.

But do encourage attendance. Publicize the highlights of the graduation ceremony, sharing your excitement at having your first, or in subsequent years, a new set of graduates. Present the event also as an opportunity for graduating students to

meet in person many of their instructors and fellow students. By planning ahead, announcing details early, and encouraging participation, probably between 50 and 60 percent of your graduating students will attend. The ceremony can contribute significantly to the creation of a lasting bond between your school and its new graduates, many of whom already are or soon will be in positions where they can help by becoming donors and referring prospective students. Make the ceremony an event that will form a pleasant and enduring memory for all.

Conferring Honorary Degrees

Graduation is also a time to award *honorary degrees* to individuals who have distinguished themselves in service to your institution or their professional fields. Taking full advantage of your right to grant honorary degrees will benefit your institution and programs, while recognizing and encouraging outstanding service.

You may wish to select as an honorary degree recipient at the first graduation someone who was especially helpful in the startup of your online school, or someone who is well recognized in the field of study you are offering. Invite the honoree to the one on-campus faculty meeting held each year, scheduled during the days immediately before graduation. Ask the honoree to participate in the meeting and to offer advice on improving your program. Continue to communicate with the recipient over time, asking for help and advice in faculty recruitment, forming partnerships, and marketing your programs. Your honorary degree recipients will be life-long friends and will help you succeed.

The Financial-Aid Office

The last of the three centralized offices upon which you

will most depend is your institution's financial-aid office. With more than half of all online students at accredited institutions receiving financial aid, your programs will impact this office almost as much as the admissions and registrar's offices. As your programs grow, the financial-aid office will probably need to add personnel to process your students' financial-aid applications.

At most institutions, financial-aid personnel do not process large volumes of requests in short time frames, and often the personnel lack the equipment and software needed for online interaction with applicants. As with applications for admission, a prolonged processing time for financial-aid applications will create uncertainties on the part of prospective students that could cause them to change their minds about registering or to enroll in another institution's online program. You will want to develop a close working relationship with the financial-aid office to ensure timely processing and that students promptly receive their award letters. Work with the office's key administrators in adapting their procedures to accommodate online students and to acquire any necessary computer equipment and software. In communicating with your students, the financial-aid office will use the students' secure institutional e-mail accounts.

You will want prospective students to have accurate information about financial aid, and an effective way to convey the information is through your Web site, using a question-and-answer format. For example:

1. If I receive financial aid but then withdraw from or drop the course for which I registered, am I required to return the financial aid?

No. You may withdraw from or drop a course, skipping the rest of term and even additional terms, without having to return the aid. Exiting the institution, however, would require you to return the aid.

"Exiting the institution" means that you give notice to the institution that you are leaving it, with no intention of registering for a future term.

2. What expenses will my financial aid cover?

Your financial aid will cover tuition, fees, textbooks, a first computer, the required software, and special assessments related to the online education. It will not pay for housing, room, board, travel, and other expenses normally associated with campus-based education, and it will not cover travel to graduation unless your institution requires attendance.

Post on your Web site the application forms for financial aid, and grant students network access so they can see internal documents related to financial aid and complete the required forms online. Set deadlines for submitting applications well before the beginning of each term so the financial-aid office will have time to complete its work. Allow about three weeks for processing and approving applications. Students desiring financial aid but who were not admitted until shortly before a term begins, or students who miss the application deadline for other reasons, will need to pay their tuition and fees with other funds while they wait for their financial-aid approvals. You will find, in fact, that many students pay by credit card or check the first term and then reimburse themselves once their financial aid arrives.

Your School's Administrators and Staff

The admissions office, the registrar's office, and the financial-aid office will be your most important sources of support services, but your online programs will also rely upon many other of your institution's centralized facilities and services, from the mail room to the library. Yet, as indicated in earlier chapters, your programs will have their own

administrators and assistants, who will comprise the staff of your school. These are:

- *Program directors* (PDs). As discussed in Chapter 3, each of your online academic programs will have a PD, a part-time employee who designs the program's curriculum; finalizes the course titles, descriptions, goals, objectives, and outcomes; and ensures that the content matrix is followed. PDs have doctorates, are widely published, and are well known in their fields. Although they have administrative functions within your school, they also serve as faculty members. As part of their training, you will want your PDs to teach at least one course early in the curriculum.

- *Faculty assistant course experts (FACEs).* The important role that FACEs play has been covered in previous chapters, mostly in Chapter 2. FACEs are information technology specialists who function primarily as an "inter*face*" between instructors and students. They convert instructors' course content and materials to Web formats, and they keep instructors on schedule. They also help students who experience technical problems, and they forward completed student assignments and other student materials to the instructors.

- *Student advisers.* The role that the student advisers play in student services and retention was discussed in Chapter 4. They are the service team for your school, helping new students adjust to the online learning experience and advising them as they progress through their courses.

- *A student counselor.* The student counselor is your primary marketing person. Information on the

student counselor's responsibilities appears earlier in this chapter and in Chapter 4. Although the counselor functions as a student recruiter, this person is your staff member, not a staff member of your institution's admissions office.

- *An executive assistant.* The position holds many responsibilities: serving as the office manager; supervising the secretarial and clerical staff; managing the business aspects of the online programs; ensuring that staff have the resources necessary to do their jobs; serving as backup to all non-academic positions; and taking on special assignments. Your executive assistant will be the glue that holds everything together.
- *Clerical staff.* These employees include secretaries, data processors, and a receptionist.

Your administrators and staff will be few initially, but their numbers will grow as more students are attracted to your programs each year. Retention of well-qualified personnel should be a priority. As stated earlier with regard to faculty persons, your goal is to recruit once and retain always.

Budgeting and Financial Planning

The intricate process of budgeting for your start-up costs and initial operations will require an accurate determination of your personnel needs and a realistic projection of registrations for your first few years. You will want to prepare detailed annual budgets for your first two years, which will take you from the planning phase well through the implementation of your first course. As part of your long-range financial planning, also prepare less detailed annual budgets for your next four years of operation, updating each year's budget on a regular

basis as your projected revenues and expenses become more certain.

The *planning phase* for your school will take from 12 to 16 months and will be all expense, no revenue. You can anticipate costs for the planning phase to be about $100,000, with the main expense being the salary and benefits of the school's chief administrator.

Your *first year* implementation budget will include additional allocations to cover the contracted fees for lead faculty persons, part-time salaries and travel expenses for program directors, and full-time salaries and benefits for one FACE and the executive assistant. You will also include in your budget the costs for your e-learning software and hosting service.

Initially, you will need one lead faculty person to develop and teach the single core course you will offer in your inaugural term, but within about two months you will need additional lead faculty persons to develop and teach the other courses you plan to offer the second term, and so on for the third and subsequent terms. Your lead faculty expenses will be very cost-effective and fairly easy to project. You will be able to base the allocation for lead faculty on the number of lead faculty persons with whom you will contract and the dollar amount of each lead faculty contract, with the norm being $3,000.

You will also need to budget during the first year of implementation for program directors, one for each degree program you offer, with the salary norm being $15,000. Include travel, meal, and lodging expenses for the PDs' visits to your institution, at least four trips annually. Also include in the budget an estimate for incentives PDs may earn by referring students to your programs.

Plan to increase your expenses by about 25 percent

annually for the first two or three years after you begin operation. During the second year of operation, you will add a full-time student adviser and a full-time student counselor. By the third or fourth year, with the expectation that registrations will double annually, both revenues and expenses will increase dramatically, but revenues will by then outpace expenses, and your school will begin to recoup its start-up costs and any annual deficits during its first years of operation.

Decide on the best time to begin using digital lead generation (DLG) in recruiting students, and in the budget for that year include the costs for the DLG contract and for the salaries and benefits of the full-time student counselor who will follow up on the DLG leads. The DLG expense can grow rapidly but pays for itself many times over as students register and begin working toward their degrees and certificates. The author calculates that his investment in DLG yielded a return of 20 to one.

Within a few years, your small budget with its few allocations will become a relatively large budget with many allocations, but it will be easier to prepare because you will be able to project revenue and expenses more accurately based on past experience and your rate of growth. The one problem you might have at that point is keeping growth in check, a problem any chief administrator would welcome.

Obtaining Your State's Authority for New Programs

Besides the requirements of your institutional accreditor, and your specialized accreditor if applicable, as discussed in Chapter 2, you will also need to consider the requirements of your state's postsecondary education agency or your state's office of degree authority. Public higher education institutions in every state are required to have state authority to grant

degrees and, in most states, private schools must also meet this requirement. Only in a few states are proprietary colleges and universities free to grant degrees without the prior approval their states.

The level of public oversight of higher learning institutions varies immensely from state to state. Some states do not closely monitor colleges and universities with accreditation by recognized accreditors because these states are primarily concerned with the schools no one else is watching. But most states do require that any college or university obtain approval before offering new programs.

Be certain of compliance with your state's higher education regulations by reviewing the information on the appropriate agency's Web site. In many states, a standardized process is in place for applying for the authority to grant new degrees, and you will be able to download the forms and instructions. Unless another institution in your state wishes to and can demonstrate that you should not be permitted to offer the new programs, you will be given the authority to grant the new degrees.

Partnerships with Other Institutions

Forming partnerships with other online schools is a simple way to increase your market share, resulting in needed revenue during the first years of your school, before your programs have had time to grow, and in extra revenue later after your registrations have reached a sustainable point.

The ease of partnering is due to the universal accessibility of online educational programs. A course can be accessed from any location, in any time zone, by any student with an Internet connection, the course identification code, and the password. Making your courses available to other institutions also benefits the partnership institutions. To form a partnership,

little more is required than the negotiation of an agreement. You can arrange with your webmaster to grant students from a partnership institution access to your courses through a splash page, complete with a calendar and course schedule that is designed to resemble the partnership school's Web site. Students will feel more comfortable in accessing their courses through a page that has their home school's look and feel.

If you plan to offer courses with an emphasis in a specialized area, they will be attractive to other institutions that do not offer them. If, for example, your courses are oriented toward health-care management, institutions that offer online business courses would be logical candidates for partnerships with your school. In contacting the chief administrators of these other campus or online schools, you would explain how their schools, by contracting for three to six of your courses, could expand their market by having a concentration in health-care management.

Finding your first partnership institution may be difficult, but those that follow will be easier. Because as many as one-third of your total registrations could be students from partnership institutions, forming partnerships can contribute significantly toward your school's financial stability. Students from partnership institutions who enroll in your courses should pay their tuition and fees directly to your school, eliminating paperwork and staff time on the part of the partnership institution.

Allow administrators of online programs at partnership institutions to preview your courses, which will make it possible for them to pre-approve the courses for transfer credit back to their institutions. Prepare periodic reports to the partnership institutions on the progress of their students. Most of all, keep lines of communication open and use them frequently. Talk

with your counterparts at partnership institutions often, being open in answering all questions.

Keeping Your Students After They Graduate

Perhaps it is appropriate from a structural standpoint that the last section of this chapter on "Administration" should cover alumni relations, but the topic is really one that deserves your attention during the implementation phase of your new online school. Either your school or your institution's alumni office will need to plan early for maintaining records on your graduates, not only for the purpose of soliciting their help with donations and student recruiting, but for tracking their successes.

Having an alumni association for your school in place by the time of your first graduation will foster your former students' continued involvement with your school. Through your school's alumni association, you can offer your former students many benefits, including e-mail accounts, newsletters with class notes, and a host of discounted services offered by companies that would view your graduates as preferred customers. From among the students due to graduate, cultivate one or two as leaders of the alumni association for that graduating class. As the years go on, the alumni association will have one or two class representatives for each group of graduates, people who will help in fund raising and maintaining your alumni network. Quite a few of your alumni, if not ignored, will become donors and help by referring future students.

Having an effective alumni relations program also gives you a way to track your graduates' successes. You will want to do this for three reasons. First, accrediting agencies, in requiring colleges and universities to demonstrate the effectiveness of their programs in light of their institutional

mission statements, consider the composite profile of a school's alumni as definitive evidence. Secondly, you can use your alumni profile, or profiles of individual alumni, in marketing your programs to prospective students. Thirdly, you will be able to identify those alumni as time goes on who warrant cultivation through personal contacts.

Staying informed on the accomplishments of your alumni requires regular contact with them through online communications and surveys. Communicate with your alumni several times a year. Tell them about the progress you are making and the changes taking place within your programs, and tell them about their peers and former instructors. Although it is true that graduates of online programs generally do not have as strong an allegiance to their alma maters as do graduates of campus-based programs, you will be able to maintain close affiliations with many long after they have taken their degrees.

6.
Software

Selecting the right software for your online programs will enhance their educational effectiveness by providing a variety of delivery formats and uniformly structuring the presentations of different courses. You will need to select two kinds of software applications. The first will be your e-learning software, an application for converting course content to online formats and then presenting the courses to students. The second software application will be for developing and managing your public Web site.

Students and instructors will also need various software programs. Additionally, depending on whether your institution has a student information system (SIS) that meets your needs, you may want to obtain your own SIS software.

Selecting an e-Learning Application

Several vendors offer e-learning software with features and prices that vary considerably. A low-cost application will not necessarily be your most cost-effective choice after operations begin due to content translation complexities and other limitations that impose demands on your FACE's time. You will want your software to be easy and economical to use, with versatility and uniformity in the ways it presents course content. You will also want to purchase the software from a reliable vendor, a stable company with a record of prompt

software support service. Finally, you want your vendor to have reliable hosting capabilities.

Prepare a comparison study of different e-learning applications by inviting several vendors to demonstrate their software. The demonstrations can take place online in real time. Among the software programs you should include in your comparison study are eCollege, Blackboard, and an open source candidate, Moodle.

Look first for an application where the navigation remains constant and consistent from course to course, a feature students will appreciate as they progress through the courses in their programs of study. Next, see if the software allows for easy content translation. Your FACE, who converts instructors' materials to Web presentations, will be able to work more efficiently, saving you staff time and preventing delays. Thirdly, be sure the software is versatile, that it offers different formatting options. Because not all course content can be effectively delivered in the same format, you will want an e-learning application that allows for visual, auditory, and print delivery of content.

Use a list of software specifications and features when reviewing the different e-learning applications, and check off the specifications and features that each application has. Your institution's information technology department can help you identify the specifications to include on your list. Doing a comparison study rather than relying on the recommendations of colleagues will ensure that your final selection will be the one best suited for the success of your programs.

Because information technology departments at higher learning institutions typically do not have the experience and capabilities for developing and supporting an e-learning program, the author does not recommend using internally developed

software. Nor is in-house hosting advisable. Outsourcing for your software and hosting services to a company whose only business is developing and hosting e-learning software will save you many hours of frustrating downtime. Contracts with vendors often cover both the software and the hosting service, with periodic fees based on the number of registrants for all courses. The rate can vary from $50 to $150 per student per course. To have the bandwidth needed for transmitting online courses yourself, your institution must have, at a minimum, a T1. Multiple T1s (OC3) are preferred.

The e-learning software used at the author's institution was provided by eCollege, and it remains the author's software of choice. Of the software applications the author compared, he found eCollege the most functional, with a major advantage being its ease of use by both students and administrators. The vendor provided the software and the Web hosting service at a per-student-per-course cost, a highly cost-effective arrangement and one that kept software and hosting expenses commensurate with the school's relatively small enrollment during its first few years. The software is tightly constructed to give the student a consistent platform from which to receive content. Throughout all courses, the software uses a uniform course format with tabs across the top and a unit division down the left side. For the student, the software becomes after only a short time an almost indiscernible element of the course presentations. The content of a course, not the delivery software, should be the visible aspect of the course being presented, and eCollege through its consistent platform presentation meets this criterion.

For your FACEs and instructors, the software's ease of use is attributable to a consistent and reproducible method for the placement of instructional presentation files and teaching materials, and for constructing links. The consistent method

of content placement reduces course production time, allowing FACEs and instructors to concentrate on the quality of content. For both staff and students, eCollege provides technical support services.

Learning to make full use of any new software takes time. The expertise your FACEs and instructors acquire should remain relevant as the e-learning software evolves with the addition of new features. In upgrading its software, eCollege has maintained its basic platform and presentation. The look and feel of the software, and the way it operates, have not changed. Some other e-learning software companies, whose applications are in the first place difficult to implement, alter their presentation platforms as they develop upgrades.

Another eCollege advantage is its hosting service. Global balancing, which allows for worldwide accessibility of content, is a necessity for educational programs that plan to attract international students, and the hosting service that eCollege offers meets this need. Outsourcing the school's hosting needs to eCollege also gave the author significant peace of mind, as eCollege has an uptime rating of 99.99 percent, making it a leader in the industry.

With its course management system, its program administrative system, its support services for students and staff, and its secure, scalable, and reliable hosting environment, eCollege would be a most suitable vendor choice for any online school.

Software for Web Site Construction and Management

Your Web site, as mentioned in previous chapters, is vital to the success of your online programs. You will want the ability to easily manage its content, so your webmaster can update

it with regularity, adding new information and removing old material.

Your webmaster will be able to construct a site that conforms to your design and layout preferences. The Web site for the author's school was constructed and maintained with Macromedia and Contribute3. The webmaster used these software applications because they ensured the consistency of specific information appearing in different places, and they allowed for ease and quickness in managing the content of the site.

At first, the main purpose of your new Web site will be to give your school a presence on the Internet, a place where prospective students and others can learn about the programs you will soon be offering. In a short time, however, your site will become a source of comprehensive information for both prospective and current students, and for faculty as well. As covered in Chapter 4, you will be placing considerable material on the site, including numerous documents and forms. To recap, the more important items for Web posting are:

1. Courses and degrees, listed with course descriptions, goals, objectives, outcomes, credit hours, generic syllabi, and each course's lead faculty person.

2. The academic degree planner.

3. A supplemental materials page, for those special downloads or software packages that are course specific or difficult to find.

4. Prospective student pages, with information that includes fact sheets about the courses or programs, admission requirements, tuition and fees, an interactive admissions application and instructions, a financial-aid application and instructions, an online inquiry form, and the e-mail address and phone number for your student recruiting counselor.

5. Your school's student and faculty handbooks in downloadable format.

6. A forms page for current students, where they can access any form they might need during their enrollment in your school.

7. Calendars, both academic and course.

8. A term-specific textbook page, with links to past terms and texts. List required textbooks for an upcoming term about 60 days in advance, and keep an archive of textbooks used in previous terms for those who wish to see if the texts have changed.

9. Links to bookstores that supply texts used in your courses.

10. Information about jobs in fields related to your programs' disciplines, with links to archived webcasts about careers. Once a term, have one of your program directors, on a rotating basis, discuss the current job outlook, including demand and salary scales, in a selected field. The webcasts will help inform students about the job market they are preparing to enter.

11. Links to archived orientation and training sessions, and to information about those upcoming.

12. Links that provide access to resources provided by your institution's library.

13. Faculty and staff pages, where program directors, lead faculty persons, and primary staff are featured.

14. A listing of partnership affiliations, to promote the relationships and to give the partnership institutions a presence on your site.

15. Your programs' mission statements, accreditation information, and organizational structure.

16. A news page, which could carry brief articles about

alumni, instructors, and staff, or about new developments with your online programs.

17. A "Contact Us" page, inviting prospective students and others to contact you and your staff. Include names, e-mail addresses, your school's mailing address, and your phone and fax numbers.

Work with your webmaster to develop a procedure for the timely updating of your site. Review the changes afterward to ensure they are free of typos and other mistakes. Your school's Web site will be, perhaps more literally so than figuratively, the window through which the world will see your school—and also appraise it.

Technology Considerations for Students

About 90 percent of all computers sold have Microsoft products installed. It makes sense, then, to have students use Microsoft software for accessing and downloading their course materials. They should have Microsoft Word, Excel, and PowerPoint. Other software programs they will need—such as Flash, Acrobat Reader, and Shockwave—are free downloads from the Internet.

Encourage students to use a high-speed Internet connection, such as cable or DSL. Quick access and fast downloading will make your courses a more satisfying experience for students. A high-speed connection is especially desirable for participation in live webcasts. However, many of your online students who had dial-up connections before enrolling will continue to use them.

Placing the student login link on your Web site's home page will require students accessing their courses to access the home page first, where they will see any new topics you have posted. Some e-learning applications require a separate login

or "splash" page. You will want to retain the right to edit this page in order to keep it current.

You will need to provide students access to your institution's local area network (LAN) so they may view and download documents and forms available from the library, financial-aid office, registrar's office, and business office. Request your institution's information technology department to assign students the same LAN user name and password that they enter in accessing their courses. Students will appreciate not having to use different login names and passwords.

Software for Faculty and Administrators

The same software programs and connections recommended for students will serve your program directors, instructors, and administrators. Most courses will use Microsoft Word as their document format, and these files are easily placed into the eCollege software.

Encourage your instructors to create and use PowerPoint presentations, incorporating audio files that explain the slides. Instructors may create one audio file per slide, using the Sound Recorder feature that is part of the Microsoft Windows operating system. One audio file per slide allows for quick editing without the need to re-record an entire presentation.

Software for a Student Information System

You may need to develop a student information system (SIS) specifically for your online school, especially if your institution does not maintain an SIS or the SIS it does have is inadequate for the type and volume of information you want to store. Having a comprehensive SIS will prove indispensable to your operations.

You can use Microsoft Access to create a database for

storing a wide array of information on each student, including demographic data, enrollment and registration information, grades, payments, and even cap and gown sizes. The database the author created contained numerous tables and hundreds of queries and reports. The software will also calculate fields, making it easy to determine GPAs, the average age of students, completion rates, the expected graduation date of a student, and much other information. The author recommends Microsoft Access if you decide to develop your own SIS.

APPENDIX A

CONTENT MATRIX SAMPLE

	COURSE 1	COURSE 2	COURSE 3	COURSE 4
CONTENT 1	X			X
CONTENT 2		X		
CONTENT 3	X		X	X

APPENDIX B

ROLL-OUT SCHEDULE

NAME & NUMBER	TITLE	FACULTY	FACE	CREDIT HOURS	START DATE	ENTER WEEKS	ENTER WEEKS	END DATE	FINAL GRADE DUE
MPH 735	Intro to Pub. Heal.	Jones	CC	4	08/29/05	***	***	11/04/05	11/18/05
MPH 745	Bio-Statistics	Brown	JH	4	08/29/05	***	***	11/04/05	11/18/05
MHA 810	Health Care Finance	Silver	SV	4	08/29/05	***	***	11/04/05	11/18/05
MHA 816	Health Care Mgmt.	Smith	DM	4	08/29/05	***	***	11/04/05	11/18/05

APPENDIX C

Master of Public Health Program

The Design and Development Process at the Author's School

In designing and developing the Master of Public Health (MPH) Program, I began with the creation of a program mission statement that was consistent with the school's and institution's mission statements. The program mission statement was broad enough to encompass the conferral of a Certificate in Public Health, which I wanted to offer for students who, for financial or other reasons, could not commit to all 11 courses that would be in the master's curriculum. In turn, I eventually developed a highly focused mission statement for each course within the program, with each mission statement supporting the program's mission statement, its goal and objectives, and its commitments. The narrow focus of the mission statements for the courses ensured concentration on the subject matter of each course.

Planning a degree program with an emphasis in public health management required extensive research, beginning with a review of similar online programs at other institutions, particularly those programs that were successful. My Internet search identified ten institutions that offered a Master of Public Health degree online. I created a spreadsheet matrix listing the institutions across the top and the courses in their curricula

down the left side. For each institution, I placed an "X" in the column under its name for the courses included in that institution's MPH program, using the format below.

	University 1	University 2	University 3	University 4
Course 1	X			X
Course 2		X		
Course 3	X		X	X

Using the matrix, I was able to identify those courses that were most common to the curricula of the various institutions. The tabulated information enabled me to decide which courses definitely to include in my curriculum and, of these courses, which would most likely be my core, or common, courses. As I began choosing the courses that I would include, the matrix gave me the assurance I was not creating an MPH program that would be *too* different from the other well-recognized and successful graduate programs in public health.

In selecting my core courses, I considered three criteria. The first was whether the course was offered in the curricula

of all or almost all institutions in the matrix. The second was whether the course provided fundamental content on which to build a knowledge base. And the third criterion was whether the course would fit well into the curriculum of at least one, and preferably both, of the two other related programs I planned to offer. The courses that met these three criteria became my core courses.

The curriculum for the highly regarded MPH degree consists of a somewhat restricted content base. Five courses are required for the degree at any institution: Bio-Statistics, Environmental Health Sciences, Epidemiology, Health Service Administration, and Social and Behavioral Sciences. As it happened, these were the core courses I selected from the matrix. It would have been necessary for them to be in the curriculum even if I had not selected them as core courses because, without any one of the five courses, an institution cannot offer an MPH. The institution could, however, offer a Master of Science in Public Health, which is a much less prestigious degree.

The matrix also helped me to determine the degree-specific courses for the MPH program. My plan was to create a 33-credit-hour degree program, and with five core courses already totaling 15 hours, I needed to identify only six additional courses. The last six courses practically identified themselves as I reviewed the matrix. From among the remaining courses most frequently represented on the matrix, I picked those that would be of the greatest interest to students.

Once all courses for inclusion in the MPH curriculum were identified, assigning content to courses using the content matrix (Appendix A) as a tracking tool, ensured that the program would meet regional accreditation requirements. The content matrix also made it easy to determine how many times specific content would be taught, and in which courses.

Later, after my school began operations, I discovered that instructors also found the content matrix extremely helpful. I encouraged instructors to interact with one another, often through live webcasts, to share their teaching methods and to discuss appropriate placement of content in the curriculum. Instructors made regular use of the content matrix in suggesting additions, deletions, and changes to content at various places in the curriculum. As a result, the instructors developed a keen awareness of the content matrix and came to see their teaching roles clearly. Those who taught courses early in the curriculum introduced topics and provided foundational information, while instructors of the later courses built upon the foundational knowledge, firmly cementing the material for the students. With the content matrix as a guide, content tracking became a means for fostering interchange not only vertically between instructors and students, but also horizontally among the instructors themselves and between instructors and administrators.

In deciding on the amount of tuition to charge per credit hour, I conducted a review of tuition for similar programs at comparable institutions. I concentrated on public health programs offered at least partially online by regionally accredited institutions that marketed their online courses to a geographically dispersed population of students, rather than to a local or regional population. My desire was to set tuition in the middle, neither at the low end nor at the high end. By placing the program in the middle of the price scale, I could expect to attract a good number of students and still have room to raise tuition if necessary.

With total credit hours, courses, content, and tuition identified, I then began recruiting faculty. I first enlisted my program directors, one for each of the three programs the

school would offer. The program directors, drawing upon their expansive networks of professional relationships, in turn recruited the faculty team. Because we were using the Just-in-Time model for course creation, not all instructors were recruited at the onset. The instructors were contracted as the courses were needed, allowing a nine-month lead time for course development. The incremental development of the courses minimized the impact on the budget.

I e-mailed the newly recruited instructors a brief survey asking about their experience and abilities in using e-mail, chat, Word, PowerPoint, Excel, file transfer protocol (FTP), and computers in general. As time went on, I learned not to be disappointed if a new instructor had little computer experience or was unfamiliar with the software applications used at our school. For these instructors, the faculty assistant course expert (FACE) provided training and assistance. Some of the best online instructors I had were ones with little computer experience when first contracted.

At the beginning of the developmental phase for each course, the FACE issued a production schedule to the lead faculty person in charge of creating the course. The schedule listed projects and tasks in reverse order, beginning with the start date for the course and working backward. The reverse order served to emphasize the completion date for all course-development work and helped define the time allocations and deadlines for finishing each project and task. Listed in chronological order, rather than the reverse sequence of the production schedule, the major projects and tasks the production schedule included were:

1. *A decision on how the course will be broken into units.* The lead faculty person for each new course first made an initial determination as to how the course would be segmented into

units. Will the online course follow the textbook chapter by chapter, with a set number of chapters per unit, or will the course be segmented by weeks, by topics, or perhaps by concepts? I found that an early decision on how a course will be divided better enabled an instructor to visualize and construct the course.

2. *Establishment of unit goals, objectives, and outcomes.* Guided by the course descriptions, goals, objectives, and outcomes developed by the administration, the lead faculty person established goals, objectives, and outcomes for each unit within the course. These were later used in assessing student learning and in evaluating the educational effectiveness of the units—to determine whether the units were truly achieving their stated purposes.

3. *Placement of course content by unit.* The lead faculty person distributed the course content over the units. For each unit, vehicles for conveying the content were identified and prepared for online display, as follows:

a. *Lectures and notes.* The instructor prepared written lectures and notes using Microsoft Word, and the FACE converted and inserted the Word files into the e-learning software. The lectures and notes—20-minute segments written in conversational language—explained and clarified textual material.

b. *PowerPoint presentations.* For more difficult material, the instructor with the FACE's help prepared PowerPoint presentations with audio overlays, with the FACE converting them to Web formats.

c. *Threaded discussions (forums).* The instructor planned the asynchronous forums for the course, listing the questions and topics to be covered.

d. *Chat sessions.* The instructor developed the agendas for the course's chat sessions.

e. *Animated Flash presentations.* For topics or content areas that lent themselves to the use of animation, the instructor and the FACE cooperated in developing Flash presentations. Accounting, statistics, and other data-intensive material are particularly well suited for Flash. The presentations can be both educational and entertaining.

f. *Video.* The instructor, conferring with the FACE, decided on any video presentations the course might include. Online students in ever greater numbers are using high-speed Internet connections, such as cable and DSL, but it was my experience that most online students are still using dial-up modems. Video, then, is a presentation vehicle to be used sparingly if at all. A video may look great on your T1 or DSL at the school, but the end student user likely has only a 56K dial-up. If video is employed in a course, the instructor should use it only for short introductions of topics, no longer than 30 seconds.

4. *Identification of evaluation tools.* All quizzes and exams were prepared, reviewed for accuracy, and finalized. Computer-graded multiple choice, true-false, matching, and short-answer tests were subjected to trial runs and the results verified.

5. *Final editing and approval.* Three weeks before the course start date, the lead faculty person submitted all course materials. The appropriate program director reviewed the content and, if no changes were in order, approved the course.

Allowing nine months for the creation of a new course gave instructors time to complete the course-development work while tending to their responsibilities at their home institutions. Additional downtime was built into the nine-month period in the event the instructor encountered unforeseen scheduling conflicts or other delays. No lead faculty person worked

continuously over the entire nine months, but each course on average did take nine months to develop.

The Teaching of the Courses

Once all course materials are ready for online presentation, the instructors and FACEs launch the courses and the teaching phase begins. The teaching of the online courses, whether from the perspective of lead faculty or adjunct faculty, is the most satisfying aspect of online educational programs. The lead faculty persons may not relish the course-development phase, but every true teacher enjoys the teaching phase.

Students engage themselves in the courses by reading their instructors' lectures and notes, participating in the forums and chat sessions, playing and replaying the PowerPoint presentations, and reading the texts. If problems exist with the online formats or hyperlinks, the students will detect them at once. Their comments and questions will indicate whether the technical aspects of a course are sound, and their level of learning, as revealed by evaluation tools, will demonstrate the course's educational effectiveness.

An online course cannot leave anything to the imagination or allow for assumptions on the part of students. Because no physical classroom exists, an instructor cannot designate material to be covered later in class. The class is online. An instructor must provide in online presentations all the information about a topic that students need in order to be successful in the course.

The most rewarding part of a new online educational program, for both faculty and administrators, is to see the time and work that went into creating a course culminate in a fulfilling experience, one where students eagerly participate in

discussions as they acquire new knowledge. And it all happens at a distance.

APPENDIX D

Master of Health Administration Program

The development of the Master of Health Administration (MHA) Program followed a process identical to that used for the Master of Public Health Program (Appendix C). The one difference in the development of the two programs was in the courses selected. The curriculum for the MHA certificate and degree program had eight core courses. The remaining courses focused on specific topics associated with health administration, including finance, health-care organization, and human resources.

The MHA is a degree for top and middle managers who work for health maintenance organizations, preferred provider organizations, insurance companies, hospitals, and health-care corporations. It is not the same graduate degree that hospital administrators typically obtained in former years. The MHA is much more detailed and extensive in its scope than any similarly titled degree conferred in the past.

An adviser to my school, who was the senior vice president of a large long-term care conglomerate, once told me he considered a master's degree to be entry-level education for all new hires. The master's degree requirement for entry to the health-care management field demonstrates the evolution that the field has undergone in recent years. The complexities that today's health-care managers face place an increased responsibility

on educational institutions to create programs that will meet the needs of employers who expect the graduates they hire to arrive with the ability to function well in a multifaceted environment.

Specialized Accreditation: Is It Required by Employers?

In Chapter 2, I discussed the obstacles associated with seeking specialized, or programmatic, accreditation. I mentioned that most specialized accreditors developed their standards with only campus-based programs in mind, and that some of the requirements of the standards, such as those that apply to facilities and services, are inappropriate for online programs. Perhaps some specialized accreditors, like the skeptical traditional educators described in Chapter 5, have doubts about whether graduate programs in their disciplines can be effectively taught online, and this may be the reason they have not amended their standards to make the requirements applicable. More often, however, the inappropriate standards of specialized accreditors are simply holdovers from pre-online times.

Because the students who would enroll in the MHA program would want assurances that they could be hired for the positions they were seeking despite the lack of specialized accreditation, I contacted numerous potential employers to ask if they required job applicants to have their MHA degrees from a school with specialized accreditation. I discovered that the employers as a rule are not concerned about whether a job applicant's degree program within a regionally accredited institution has specialized accreditation. The only instance I found where the degree must be from a program with specialized accreditation was for military advancement in a health-care setting. All other employers answered that they

were most interested in the candidate's ability to perform well in the position. Specialized accreditation of the program from which the candidate had earned a master's degree was not a requirement for being hired. As the shortest time-to-degree program, with a very competitive tuition and an all-online format, students thought my programs were ideal for them. The student count doubled each year. As graduates advance in their careers and employers who are looking for performance are pleased, I believe it is reasonable to expect a similar if not greater rate of enrollment growth in the future.

APPENDIX E

Master of Geriatric Health Management Program

The planning, design, and development of the Master of Geriatric Health Management (MGH) Program was a unique endeavor. Unlike the two other programs described in Appendices C and D, the MGH program had no precedents at other institutions. As an altogether new degree, I could not draw upon the curricula of other online programs in selecting courses, except for the core courses. The design and content for the additional courses had to be developed independently, without the benefit of existing models. The guide for planning the new courses, as with the other two programs, was the program's mission statement, which encompassed preparing students for management positions at long-term care facilities and community-based health services agencies for the elderly.

Long-Term Care Management

Certainly, many different kinds of facilities had been providing long-term care for older adults long before my school made the decision to develop the MGH program. But the management aspect of long-term care facilities and community-based health services agencies for the elderly was changing. The decision to create the new degree was based on the fact that geriatric health management, with the dramatic

growth of the industry and the emergence of many interwoven community resources and care systems, had become a complex process. The new degree program was undertaken in the belief that long-term care management now warranted the emphasis that a separate program would provide. As one of my program directors told me, the extent of his exposure to long-term care management while he was working on his MHA was but a small part of one course. That had been only a few years earlier.

Today, several national conglomerates provide long-term care for many thousands of the elderly. The care facilities are diverse, ranging from single-story ranch-style retirement communities in the West to high-rise towers in the East. In between are freestanding nursing homes, assisted-living centers, and in-home care services. Additionally, adult-day-care and respite-care services are offered at the private homes of the elderly by various companies and organizations. With this diversity in facilities and services, the era of "vertical integration" for geriatric health management has arrived (Pratt, 2004): The typical geriatric health-care conglomerate now owns hospitals, post-hospital convalescent and rehabilitation facilities, nursing homes, adult day-care centers, and in-home care services.

The long-term care manager today must be a professional who is proficient in finance, accounting, law, ethics, human resources, organizational structures, economics, and state-of-art medical care. My school was an early responder to the burgeoning need for well-trained long-term care managers. At the time, a degree program with an emphasis in geriatric health management was unique, but many other institutions since then have also responded. The need for effective managers in this field, however, has not diminished. Because the "boomers" of the 1940s will be, in the not-very-distant future,

our country's elderly, the demand for well-trained managers in geriatric health will only increase.

Health-Care Delivery Systems for the Elderly

An overview of one course in the MGH program illustrates the unique content and structure typical of the new courses developed for the program. The intent of this course, entitled Health-Care Delivery Systems for the Elderly, was to provide students with a working knowledge of the continuum of care. It began with the history of geriatric health care and a survey of the present-day services for the elderly around the world. The course then covered the variety of services offered within the continuum of care. Each week, different levels of care and their settings were discussed, including adult day care, respite care, assisted living, and nursing-home care.

As the course progressed, students learned about the kinds of professionals and para-professionals that provide geriatric care. The thrust of the later part of the course was toward efficient interdisciplinary professional practice. Long-term care is unique in that it requires a commitment over an extended period of time to the patient or client by an interdisciplinary team. The team may include a physician, a nurse, a social worker, a physical therapist, and an occupational therapist. It should also include a para-professional who is providing daily care, a family member, and the care recipient. In short, the team is composed of everyone directly involved in providing care.

A care team is more effective when its members understand the expertise that the other members bring to the team. This understanding promotes mutual respect and cooperation, creating an atmosphere where the team as a whole can be confident in drawing upon the expertise of one member

whom the other team members know is best qualified for a specific situation or task. Since the care team includes the paraprofessional, a family member when possible, and the care recipient, a mechanism must be in place to ensure that their recommendations and suggestions are solicited and heard. A principal investigator for a recent research project involving a large number of nursing homes noted that many registered nurses, licensed nurse practitioners, and nurse's aides reported they were not included in the decision-making process (Creedon et al, 2003).

The last part of the course presented the outlook for the future: the demographic changes that lie ahead, the demands that the changes will impose, and the likely course of public policy and regulation.

A subsequent course on Administration of Long Term Care covered legal issues, personnel requirements, financial management, and reporting requirements. Not all geriatric care facilities are heavily regulated. Assisted-living facilities, for example, have relatively few reporting requirements. Nursing homes, on the other hand, are very heavily regulated, despite the objections that many nursing-home administrators have to the extensive reporting obligations placed on them (Tellis-Nayek, 2002). A good knowledge of state and federal regulatory requirements is essential for today's nursing-home administrators. They must be prepared for the regulatory requirements of their care level. They must also deal with an ever-changing workforce, with turnover rates as high as 100 percent annually for many facilities. How can administrators enhance employee morale? How can employee retention rates be improved? How can a facility improve its image in the eyes of its community? These are just some of the issues facing today's nursing-home administrators.

The Future of Long-Term Care

Many experts suggest that long-term care will soon see an increased emphasis on home care, owing almost entirely to the sheer cost of institutional care but also due to the desires of the boomer elders and their families. Degree programs in geriatric health management will need to expand their emphasis to include case management, with a focus on bringing appropriate levels of in-home care services to the elder. Geriatric health managers will need skills in assessing client needs, consultation with the client's family, and the use of home-care technologies. A new synthesis of institutional and community care is rapidly becoming a necessity, and schools that offer the Master of Geriatric Health Management degree will need to adapt their curricula in response to this new era of elder care.

References

Pratt, John R. Long Term Care: Managing Across the Continuum. Second Ed. Jones & Bartlett, Pub., Sudbury, Mass. 2004.

Creedon, M.A., Fulmer, K. A., Barbee, D. E., Lancaster, A. "Veterans Homes at the Crossroads: Final Report." Armed Forces Veterans Homes Foundation. Suitland, MD. October, 2003.

Tellis-Nayak, V. "Home Administrator Survey." November, 2002. Appendix, "Veterans Homes at the Crossroads: Final Report." October, 2002.

5761159R0

Made in the USA
Lexington, KY
12 June 2010